the series on school reform

Patricia A. Wasley
Bank Street College of Education

Ann Lieberman
NCREST

Joseph P. McDonald
New York University

SERIES EDITORS

This series also incorporates earlier titles in the Professional Development and Practice Series

One Kid at a Time

BIG LESSONS FROM A SMALL SCHOOL

Eliot Levine

FOREWORDS BY
TED SIZER
TOM PETERS

AFTERWORD BY
DENNIS LITTKY AND
ELLIOT WASHOR

TEACHERS
COLLEGE
PRESS

Teachers College, Columbia University
New York and London

To Madge, Jesse, and Cassie

Published by Teachers College Press, 1234 Amsterdam Avenue, New York, NY 10027

The research reported in this book was assisted in part by a grant from The Spencer Foundation. The data presented and the views expressed are solely the responsibility of the author.

Library of Congress Cataloging-in-Publication Data

Levine, Eliot.
    One kid at a time : big lessons from a small school / Eliot Levine ; with
forewords by Tom Peters, Ted Sizer, and an afterword by Dennis Littky
and Elliot Washor.
        p. cm. — (The series on school reform)
    Includes bibliographical references and index.
    ISBN 0-8077-4154-X (cloth : alk. paper) — ISBN 0-8077-4153-1
(pbk. : alk. paper)
        1. Metropolitan Regional Career and Technical Center (Providence, R.I.)   2. Open plan
schools—Rhode Island—Providence—Case Studies.   3. High schools—Rhode
Island—Providence—Case studies.   4. Group work in education—Rhode
Island—Providence—Case studies.   5. Educational change—Rhode
Island—Providence—Case studies.   I. Title.   II. Series.
    LD7501.P9 L495 2001
    373.745′2—dc21   2001035574

ISBN 0-8077-4153-1 (paper)
ISBN 0-8077-4154-X (cloth)

Printed on acid-free paper

Manufactured in the United States of America

09   08   07   06   05   04   03   02   8   7   6   5   4   3   2   1

Contents

Foreword from the World of Education

I'm 16. My high school is a big, crowded building. I have to stay inside it until I earn "off-campus privileges." Since I'm a kid, the adults expect that I'll cut corners, especially because I'm in the Curriculum III track. And they treat me accordingly. "Do you have a hall pass, kid?" I hate the security guys.

My classes are 47 minutes long. I go to seven in a row (with 20 minutes out for lunch). I don't talk up much in classes, because mostly I'm just supposed to listen carefully and answer questions. My teachers are nice, and they care about me, but they have very busy jobs. They don't usually have time to get to know me very well. I have a guidance counselor too, and I like her. But she hustles me out of her office when I start blabbing too much, reminding me that she has 249 other kids to counsel.

Even though I get "promoted" each year—from 9th through 12th grade—no one really knows what I learned last year or what exactly I still need to learn. That's because the curriculum is so complicated and changes all the time, and because my different teachers never seem to talk about me with each other. I just do what each teacher says, and each class is pretty much separate from the others.

We take lots of standardized tests, but they're not very hard. We spend lots of class time learning how to outsmart multiple choice questions and fill in bubble sheets. As though that's what life's all about. What a joke.

Ted Sizer is the founder of the Coalition of Essential Schools, a former dean of the Harvard Graduate School of Education, and a former teacher and principal. He is the author of several books, including *Horace's Compromise: The Dilemma of the American High School* (1984).

I like school, though. It's fun most of the time, and I don't have to work very hard. Plus there's lots of time to hang out with my friends when I can get away with it. School is much different from my job. I have to work hard there. My bosses give me responsibility. Recently they have even asked my advice on how to make our work better. They make me feel grown up.

I admit that I do get scared about the future. I know that I'm not learning much that I can use to get a good job, or to go to college. I feel that I'm just going through growing up. It's fun, I suppose. I don't complain. I pretend. But O my God what lies ahead?

Such is a familiar litany. The "grammar" of high school (as David Tyack has aptly put it)—the daily schedule, the atomized curriculum, the overworked staff, the colorful rituals of high school—seems immutable. Over the last three decades, many have dolefully described the American secondary school and its anonymity and inefficiencies, but few have made sustained efforts on the ground to change these root and branch. This is no surprise as high schools are complicated places where everything important connects with everything else and many long-established practices, of whatever educational merit, have powerful symbolic value. One messes with these at one's peril.

Dennis Littky and Elliot Washor have twice taken the risk of reform, first at Thayer High School in Winchester, New Hampshire, and more recently in Providence, Rhode Island, at the Metropolitan Regional Career and Technical Center (The Met). It is this latter effort that is the subject of this book. The volume's title signals the school's priority: Each student will be known well and taught and counseled as an individual, not as one of a class of agemates who, given the tremendous student loads on teachers and counselors, are batch processed.

Every Met student has an internship or job in the "real world." Academic goals are clear and demanding, and each student approaches these in his or her own way and speed. Graduation follows publicly demonstrated mastery. The Met tackles a swath of time-honored but ineffective practice—and the attitudes that accompany it—with daring, determination, and remarkable success.

Needless to say, Littky's and Washor's work has not been easy. Eliot Levine's chronicle and analysis spells out the difficulties, the confrontations, the compromises, and the victories. He tells a story that all Americans who are impatient with the pace of serious reform of schools must read and ponder carefully. One Kid at a Time. It is possible. It works.

Theodore R. Sizer

"Business Guy"
Foreword

This is not a foreword! It is a fan letter!

Years ago, Chester Nimitz, the admiral who won the Pacific War for the U.S., was listening to a presentation by a young man. Afterwards he sidled up to the fellow, and asked to have their picture taken together. Asked why, he replied that he wanted, years in the future, to have been seen standing next to this young world beater.

That's me. I want the record formally to note that I "stood beside" this incredible-imaginative-passionate tale of how America's educational approach can be reformed. (Though I hate myself when the word "reform" oozes out of my brain and on to paper. It recalls "modern" school reform . . . one of our nation's greatest embarrassments.)

Warren Bennis—scholar, leadership guru, former university president—is the only person on earth who is close to both Peter Drucker (the management uber-guru) and me. Asked by a reporter about the two of us, Warren replied, "If Peter 'invented' modern management, Tom repainted it in Technicolor." I loved that! And I hope it contains a grain of truth.

When Bob Waterman and I penned *In Search of Excellence*, America was under economic frontal assault by Japan. Our post-WWII invincibility was anything but. A lot of the fault lay beside the Charles River, at the Harvard Business School. That, of course, is not fair to Harvard; but the Harvard-MBA-Strategic Planning dogma of the time had reduced "management" to a dry, by-the-

Tom Peters delivers management seminars worldwide and is the author or co-author of seven bestselling books, including *In Search of Excellence* (1982) and *Liberation Management* (1992).

numbers exercise . . . reminiscent of the current teach-to-test malaise in education. Bob and I roamed the nation, looking at companies that worked, and we saw something else. "It" was "soft," by the Charles River Standard. It had to do with people & engagement in the work & love of quality & entrepreneurial instincts & values worth going to the mat for. We wrote about it, and to our delight and dismay the world listened.

"The world listened" . . . not because of the scintillating prose . . . but because the competitive situation demanded it. Our wild "stuff" has now become commonplace: Engage your folks. Make things that are cool and that work. Stick your neck out. Now, in business, you could almost say that . . . Passion Rules! Our leading business strategist at the millennium's start, Gary Hamel, offers this as his #1 rule for success: *"Create a 'cause,' not a 'business'."*

The Met is a cause worth signing up for . . . and emulating. It is founded on one word: *engagement*. The "engaged" kid learns. The dis-engaged kid doesn't. It's damn near as simple as that. What Met gurus Dennis Littky and Elliott Washor call LTI (learning through internships) is nothing more and nothing less than a formula for engagement: Create a cause, not pursuit-of-rote-learning-to-no-useful-end-other-than-good-SATs-that-get-Johnny-into-Harvard. (Okay, I'll stop picking on Harvard. What do you expect from a Stanford guy?)

Here's the deal, the "business-guy case." This is what I write about these days, condensed from 100,000 words to a coupla hundred. (It's okay to write "coupla," even if the ETS would lambaste me for it.) There is a work revolution underway. Led by New Technology, led by the Internet . . . I confidently predict that 90% of white collar jobs (which are 90% of all jobs these days), including teaching "jobs," will disappear or be reconfigured beyond recognition within 10 to 15 years. It'll be bigger than the farm-to-factory tsunami of 1750+. MIT recently reported, for instance, that less than 50% of us will be employed as full-time workers by 2010. In an incredible new book, *Free Agent Nation*, author Daniel Pink claims that already 31–55 million of us are in something akin to the "independent contractor" mode of professional being.

Consequence of "all this"? Michael Goldhaber, writing in *WIRED*, says, ***"If there is nothing very special about your work, no matter how hard you apply yourself, you won't get noticed,*** *and that increasingly means you won't get paid much either."* I call that the #1 Tough Love quote of all time for adults!

My response? A coupla books in a series we dubbed The Work Matters. *The Brand You50: Fifty Ways to Transform Yourself from an "Employee" into a Brand that Shouts Distinction, Commitment, and Passion!* and *The Project50: Fifty Ways to Transform Every "Task" into a Project that Matters!* That is . . . professional survival . . . as the white collar robots (new software) usurp rote jobs . . . depends on distinction and passion. Cool stuff! 100% of the time! Or else! Our "little" slogan for all this: **DISTINCT . . . OR EXTINCT.**

I'd guess you now see why I call this short essay a fan letter rather than a foreword. The (incredible, innovative, awesome) approach The Met is taking plays 100.00000% into the New Economy/ New Paradigm-of-Work picture I'm painting. I love Learning Through Internships! I love Work That Matters! I love WOW Projects! I love LOVE . . . and engagement and passion and commitment and The Technicolor Life. (Which, of course, is why I so heartily detest the SAT and teach-to-test and standardization crap that marks the counter-productive school reform movement.) (Hint: Economic value—in this age of "intellectual capital"—will spring from passion and untrammeled creativity . . . words I've never heard spring for any traditional "reformer's" lips.) (Hint: If you elect me as your President in 2004, the first thing I'll do is spend 1% of our GDP on putting the arts front and center in the school curriculums of America. Okay, okay, I'm a Howard Gardner, "multiple intelligences" fan, too.)

One final word about my journey of the last 20 years. Bob Waterman and I coined a phrase way back when: **SOFT IS HARD. HARD IS SOFT**.

It's the by-the-numbers "stuff" that's abstract and lifeless. (Hard is soft.) It's the people & passion stuff that moves mountains. King. Gandhi. Steinem. Picasso. Einstein. (Soft is hard.) My friends & colleagues, The Met ain't soft! **Look at the learning criteria and accountability measures discussed in this book . . . and weep. WOW!** I'm not at all sure I could earn a diploma from The Met, despite my consistent 800 math boards way back when. The Met demands engagement. Results. Proof of results. The ability to persuade others based on the presentation of those results. The Met = Real Life 101.

(Short story: I taught at the Stanford B-School in the early 80s. "Straight" course on "Excellent Companies." Except that I had my students evaluate a business as their team project. They offered up written reports, which I demanded; but they also had to make a 20-minute presentation to their peers and me and the business boss in my classroom. The 20-minute presentation counted for 50% of their semester grade. I told 'em it was Real Life 101, three months of grueling work that depends on a 20-minute spiel to The Client. My test-maestro students were appalled . . . but I'm still getting letters, 20 years later, and from the Real Real World, thanking me in retrospect for the exercise.)

This is a Great Book. A great piece of research. A Great Story. Will The Met Model sweep the world off its feet? I wish. With deserved help from the Gates Foundation (you go, Billy-non-Harvard-graduate), maybe so. Frankly, the odds are long, given the wrong-headed nature of The Establishment's retro approach to education. But there *is* a learning revolution going on. The Internet is leading it. So, interestingly, are talent-strapped corporations, looking for new ways to inculcate an ethos of life-long learning into their corporate "cultures." We're gonna get this damned thing done, by hook or by crook, and The Met Model . . . learning through passion for the task . . . will be front and center . . . come hell **AND** high water.

Yrs. truly, A Fan.

Tom Peters

Acknowledgments

To everyone at the Met and The Big Picture Company, I offer my gratitude. Your vision, devotion, and courage are the basis of this book. I hope that I have done justice to your stories.

The staff, students, parents, and mentors of the Met patiently answered my questions for 2 years and invited me to watch their learning unfold. My thanks are due to Charly Adler, Cheryl Barboza, Joe Battaglia, Amy Bayer, Rachel Brian, Anita Davis, Nancy Diaz, Danique Dolly, Ely Garcia, Kim Hauge, Chris Hempel, Jill Homberg, Millie Marrero, Brian Mills, Jill Olson, Roni Phipps, Phil Price, Nanette Nuñez, Charlie Plant, Lois Smith, Rick Solomon, Suzette Thibeault, Ted Tuttle, Kristin Waugh, Scott Weber, Wayne Woods, and the students, parents, and mentors whose names have been changed to protect their privacy.

The staff, consultants, collaborators, and friends of The Big Picture Company also welcomed me into their community and supported my research in countless ways. My thanks are due to Farrell Allen, Gigi DiBello, Joe DiMartino, John Fitzgerald, Stanley Goldstein, Pamela Greene, Betsy Guerzon, Elaine Hackney, Christine Heenan, Kerry E'lyn Larkin, George Lewis, Lani Shumway Macleod, Charles Mojkowski, Tom Peters, Ted Sizer, Elizabeth Wilson Rood, Molly Schen, Elayne Walker-Cabral, Laura Westberg, Cal Wolk, and Ron Wolk. Adria Steinberg and Julie Gainesburg generously allowed me to quote from and adapt their case studies of Met students.

Dennis Littky and Elliot Washor, co-directors of the Met and The Big Picture Company, supported my research from the day I knocked on their door. We spoke weekly for almost 2 years, including many lengthy interviews. It has been a privilege to work closely with two pioneers whose lives are a struggle for social justice through education reform.

Carol Weiss and Katherine Merseth of the Harvard Graduate School of Education designed and directed the fellowship program that supported my research and writing. Mary Askew, Mary Jo Bane, and Vito Perrone provided additional mentorship and support. My deep gratitude is due to the Spencer Foundation for funding my research fellowship, and to all of the faculty and associates of the Harvard Children's Initiative who supported my work.

For their encouragement and insightful feedback after reading drafts of the book, I am indebted to Bennett Brown, Madge Evers, Christine Heenan, Jill Homberg, Herb Kohl, Dennis Littky, John Lombard, Lilly Lombard, Vito Perrone, Roni Phipps, Seymour Sarason, Molly Schen, Ted Sizer, Elayne Walker-Cabral, and Elliot Washor.

Teachers College Press provided valuable guidance in framing and editing the manuscript. I am grateful to Catherine Bernard, Carole Saltz, Leyli Shayegan, Lori Tate, David Strauss, and the rest of the staff for their devotion in bringing the book to publication.

Much like students at the Met, I have been blessed with a wealth of mentors, role models, and co-conspirators whose support and activism over the years enabled me to envision and write this book. My heartfelt thanks are due to Barbara and Earle Levine (my parents), Jimmy Levine, Gordy McIntosh, Donald Perlstein, Jackie Simonis, Yoshua Leavitt, Bill McAuliffe, Paul Breer, Jim 1082, George Albee, Gloria Levin, Ed Trickett, Eric Wish, and Heather Weiss.

Finally, my wife Madge Evers supported me every step of the way, and our beautiful son Jesse has been a fountain of joy. I can't imagine having written this book without their companionship and inspiration. And to Cassie, who just arrived, welcome!

Introduction

When Cesar was in ninth grade, his career ambition was to become an assassin. His credentials were impressive—urban gang member, hardened street fighter, handgun aficionado. Dozens of his friends and family were in prison, dead, or on their way, and even his mother was resigned to his downfall. Three years later, he was a captivating poet with a scholarship to a private college.

Julia was an honor roll student who started high school a year early and quickly proved herself as a budding scientist. By age 16 she had done liver cancer research at a teaching hospital, developed gene therapy products with a biotech startup, and studied immunology at Brown University. Now she's at college working toward becoming a pediatrician.

Cesar and Julia were in the first graduating class of the Metropolitan Regional Career and Technical Center (the Met), a unique public high school in Providence, Rhode Island. The Met has no classes, no grades, no tests, and no easy rides. With guidance from adults, each student builds a customized education focused on five learning goals: communication, social reasoning, empirical reasoning, quantitative reasoning, and personal qualities.

Students spend 2 days per week at internships that they select based on their interests. One student interned with a conservation group, where she lobbied for a recycling bill, developed an anti-pollution pamphlet, and studied the biochemistry of water testing. The following 2 years her internships focused on architecture and health care. But the Met is not a vocational school; the goal is to create versatile, motivated learners—not to prepare students for specific careers.

The Met has little in common with most schools. Students study fewer topics but in far more depth. Rather than learning only with same-age peers, they also work closely with adults inside and outside of school. Instead of taking tests, they give public exhibitions of what they've learned. And instead of letter grades, they receive detailed narratives written by their teachers. Each student's learning team—teacher, parents, student, and internship mentor—meets quarterly to assess the student's progress and plan the next quarter's activities.

Relationships are the Met's foundation. Fourteen students and a teacher form a tightly knit group called an "advisory" that stays together for all 4 years of high school. Teachers have primary responsibility only for the 14 students in their advisory, so they come to know each student deeply and can accommodate different learning styles. Unlike teachers at most schools, Met teachers have time to help all of their students with even the toughest academic and personal problems.

Sounds expensive. But the Met has a public school budget and affords its unique structure primarily by reducing the number of specialty staff: librarians, guidance counselors, vice-principals, reading specialists, art and music teachers, and others. These jobs are carried out by a smaller number of staff, all of whom take on multiple roles. The school also takes advantage of many outside resources, including parents, community members, and local organizations.

The Met is the brainchild of two seasoned educators. Elliot Washor is an educational jack-of-all-trades whose work has spanned more than 20 years as a teacher, administrator, and video producer. He has taught many subjects at the elementary, secondary, and college levels, and his innovative reforms have been recognized by an award from Harvard's Kennedy School of Government.

Dennis Littky was a distinguished and controversial principal for 20 years before coming to Rhode Island. Under his leadership, a rural New Hampshire high school raised graduation rates from 80% to 98% and college attendance from 10% to 50%, but Dennis was fired by the school board for his unorthodox methods. He won his job back after a legal battle that reached the state Supreme Court, and in 1993 he was voted New Hampshire Principal of the Year. His efforts were chronicled in the book *Doc: Dennis Littky's Fight for a Better School* (Kammeraad-Campbell, 1989) and the movie *A Town Torn Apart* (NBC, 1992).

In 1994, Dennis and Elliot accepted positions at Brown University's Annenberg Institute for School Reform. They quickly recruited a talented staff and developed a broad coalition of supporters who helped them gain oversight of a new regional school that had been financed by the state. The school's design was not yet finalized, so they submitted a design proposal to the state Board of Regents, revised it as required, and received funding by a vote of the state legislature. The Met opened in 1996 and grew in phases by accepting 50 new ninth graders each year. Now the school has 200 students in grades 9–12 and will grow to 700 once the campus is fully constructed.

Dennis and Elliot are aligned with Progressivism, the century-old philosophy that students learn best by confronting problems that arise while doing things they find interesting. Those problems then become a springboard for more formal learning (Dewey, 1938/1963). Progressive ideas have at times been misinterpreted to mean that students should be allowed to do whatever they want, but Met students must pursue specific learning goals and requirements, and their progress is monitored closely by their teachers and learning teams.

Progressive ideas have gained momentum in recent years. The most prominent example is the Coalition of Essential Schools, founded by Ted Sizer, a former dean of the Harvard Graduate School of Education. In the 1980s, Sizer hand-picked Dennis Littky to be one of the Coalition's first principals. Now the Coalition has 1,000 schools nationwide, and the Met's design deeply reflects its roots in that movement. Sizer was also the Annenberg director who brought Dennis and Elliot to Providence.

The Met's student body is 41% White, 38% Latino, 18% African-American, and 3% Asian-American. Half qualify for subsidized lunch because of low family income. Most live in Providence, but by law 25% come from towns and cities across the state. One out of four Met parents has a college degree, including some with middle-class incomes and white-collar jobs. Few of these parents would ordinarily send their child to an inner-city high school, but they value the Met's approach to learning. Four staff members, including Elliot Washor, send their own children to the school.

The Met's initial successes have been remarkable. Every student in the first graduating class was accepted to college, even though more than half will be the first in their family ever to attend. And compared with other Providence high schools, the Met has just one-third the dropout rate, one-third the absentee rate, and one-eighteenth the rate of disciplinary suspensions.

This book introduces a new approach to learning. Chapter 1 chronicles the learning journeys of three diverse Met students. Chapters 2–8 explore the Met's unique mix of learning strategies. Chapter 9 assesses the Met's effectiveness, and Chapter 10 discusses the challenges of adapting the Met's principles to other schools. The book ends with a glimpse of graduation and an afterword by Met co-directors Dennis Littky and Elliot Washor.

I conducted the research for this book during a fellowship at the Harvard Graduate School of Education, funded by the Spencer Foundation. Dennis and Elliot spoke to me with remarkable candor in dozens of interviews and put no restrictions on my access to the school. For 2 years I shadowed teachers, visited internships, attended events, roamed the halls, reviewed school records, and had hundreds of discussions with students, staff, parents, and internship mentors. Few schools, even well-established ones, have ever invited such intensive scrutiny and public reporting from an external researcher; for an iconoclastic (and hence vulnerable) start-up school to have done so is extraordinary.

The Met's openness reflects the school's mission to become a catalyst for widespread reform. Shortly after Dennis and Elliot came to Providence, they formed a nonprofit organization called The Big Picture Company whose first project was designing the Met. Their most recent initiative, funded by a $3.4 million grant from the Gates Foundation, is to develop 12 schools across the country based on the Met's learning principles. The Big Picture Company has also established a K–8 charter school in Providence and a training program for school principals. Over time, their goal is to make American education more relevant, equitable, personalized, and humane.

The Met's innovations have sharpened the cutting edge of school reform. With a rare synergy of heart, expertise, and high-level public backing, the school models the informed risk-taking and honest self-evaluation that American education needs. The Met discredits the popular notion that change must be gradual (while students in the pipeline get left behind), and it fights for the best education for all students from all backgrounds. The Met's ambitious reforms and early successes merit a careful look from everyone interested in improving education.

1 Portraits of Three Students

Tamika, Julia, and Cesar were in the Met's first graduating class. Early in their junior year I selected them for in-depth portraits, because they reflected the diverse personal and academic profiles of Met students. They also showed three typical pathways through the Met, including a student whose graduation prospects were in doubt when my research began.

Shaking Off Gravity: Tamika's Story

"It's amazing what Tamika has learned," says Met co-director Elliot Washor. "Back in ninth grade she really believed in her dream of becoming a famous singer, but she didn't realize that she had no idea how to get there."

To encourage Tamika's passions, the Met invited her to compose the school song. For several months she wrote lyrics and music, trained backup singers, and cut demo tapes. Then she performed the song at a school assembly and explained the recording process to her fellow students.

For the first time, Tamika was excited about learning. In middle school she was absent 20 days per year, but at the Met she never missed more than 2. "I hardly paid attention back then," she says. "I hated getting out of bed, and I didn't feel like many teachers really cared. At the Met it's more like a family, and I always know that they're going to support me and help me move up."

Tamika's mother spoke with me in the family's apartment in South Providence. She had just completed a nursing assistant course, her first schooling since 10th grade when Tamika was born. She hopes nursing will finally be her ticket off the welfare roles.

1

"School is important," she says, "because if my kids don't go they'll be just as dumb as me. I never want them to go through what I went through. I'm so proud of what Tamika's doing in school now. The Met changed her whole life. It inspired her and prospered her. It lit up a whole bunch of things that was inside her that just come out."

"In the beginning Tamika had desire—and that's about it," says her teacher Marcus. "She's the oldest child from an African-American, single-parent household, and she's trying to bring herself and her family into a better situation."

Marcus and the other teachers help students develop projects based on their interests. Known as LTIs (for "Learning Through Internships"), these projects put students in real-world settings that motivate them to learn academic and personal skills.

Tamika's ninth-grade LTI with a repertory theater was disappointing, because the director was too busy to provide solid mentorship. Then in 10th grade, a local actress, singer, and playwright introduced her to the demanding behind-the-scenes work of being a self-employed entertainer and community activist. It was an important stepping-stone to the ambitious projects that followed. "Flora sparked a lot of hope in me," Tamika says. "We both come from not-so-hopeful backgrounds, so seeing how she's prospered, I feel like I can do it too. That's what she always told me. We still keep in touch."

As a junior and senior, Tamika collaborated with several students and mentor Joyce Golden to create their own community service organization. Teen Outreach started out with no money and no place to meet other than Golden's living room. Within 18 months they had won $80,000 in grants, rented office space, hired Golden as full-time director, and reached 1,000 youth with their cultural and educational programs. Tamika was deeply involved in all aspects of the process.

"At first Tamika was always losing things and struggled to get her point across," Golden says. "Now she has directed a complex event attended by 90 people. After deciding on a theme—the impact of African-American culture on our society—she did a timeline, booked performers, managed publicity and rehearsals, and supervised six youth assistants. The next year, for her senior project at the Met, she created an intensive support group for at-risk middle-school girls. Her work has been phenomenal."

After 4 years of working with Tamika, her teacher, Marcus, has developed a deep understanding of her abilities and learning style. This helps him make effective decisions about her education. She needs to work harder at math, for example, but would rather focus on Teen Outreach. Marcus helps her learn how to manage these competing demands. He sees them as complementary, because skills Tamika developed at Teen Outreach helped her succeed in a college algebra course. But striking a balance has been difficult, and Marcus fears that she will struggle with math in the future.

Tamika's language skills have been a more clear-cut victory. "Wuz up, how ya doing," she wrote in ninth grade. "Me I'm doing good. My toes was frozen on New Years. Time pases madd quick." Just 3 years later she speaks with phrases such as "We've built a relationship with the United Way" and "Our capacity is big compared to the size of our office."

Real-world projects like Teen Outreach motivated Tamika to improve her skills. "When you're asking a philanthropist for money," her mentor explains, "you have to say 'Yes, I agree,' not 'Yo, dat's buttahs.' Tamika learned those unwritten rules quickly. She has also become a serious writer. For Teen Outreach, she has written grant applications, press releases, and newsletters. Then back at the Met she gets lots of help with editing. You can't compare her writing to what it was before."

Marcus agrees, but he is wary of complacency. "I'm happy," he says, "but I can't get too happy. She's doing great now, but it would be too easy for her to rest on her laurels. She's got plenty of things she needs to work on. I always keep that in mind, and I keep on pushing."

"Who knows what would have happened to Tamika at another school?" muses Met co-director Dennis Littky. "Maybe she would have been a B or C student who did fine in college. Or maybe she would have dropped out and gotten completely lost. But she definitely wouldn't have become a shining star with her own non-profit organization and so many relationships with adults who care deeply about her. She wouldn't have won a $10,000 scholarship for outstanding community service. And she wouldn't have ended up where she's headed now—an Ivy League university with a full scholarship. Few schools have the time to pick up on the potential of students like Tamika. She still lacks some skills and confidence at times, but she has become a different person. Now her potential is to do anything she wants."

Birkenstocks and Biotech: Julia's Story

Julia dispels the myth that the Met is only for students with few options and little to lose. Her suburb is home to the state's top-ranked high school, but she and her parents chose the Met (and a 10-mile commute) instead. A shy honors student, Julia skipped eighth grade and entered the Met at age 13.

"Julia loves animals and science," says her teacher, Emily. "Her first project was trying to elicit a Pavlovian response from two mice. She forgot to include a control group, so it was hard to draw conclusions, but she really started to understand what it means to do science. Giving students the freedom to make mistakes is an important part of learning."

Julia planned to become a veterinarian, so she arranged an LTI studying penguin development at the zoo. She learned about spreadsheets, graphing, research methods, and teamwork. "It was great," Emily says, "because she had to stop hiding behind books and really work with people. We used to joke that I was always yelling at her for reading. When her mentors asked her to redo her report from scratch, she was incredibly frustrated—but that's the real world."

In a traditional classroom Julia would have received a B+ and never taken another look at her report, but for the research lab she had to revise and revise until her work met professional standards. Eventually her data became part of a presentation at a scientific conference.

The next year Julia did her LTI at Rhode Island Hospital. At first she attended brain dissections and inspected the slices with pathologists. Later she edited autopsy transcripts and wrote pamphlets for brain donors. Then she worked with Linda Carver, a doctoral student doing liver cancer research.

"We were discussing immunofluorescent markers on Julia's first day," Linda says, "and I mentioned the blocking stage that comes after adding the first antibody. Out of the blue Julia asked, 'Is that so the second antibody won't interact with one that's still unbound?' And my jaw dropped. I mean, that was the whole point. She is very intelligent, and her project was a great help. It was something I was going to have to do myself."

In 11th grade, Julia did gene-therapy research with a biotech company. They had high expectations because of her lab experience and the three biology courses she had taken at Brown University. It was stressful for Julia, because her work affected the company's bottom line and she had to learn their complicated lab procedures.

Julia's learning at the Met has also included community service projects and outdoor leadership activities. Because of partial hearing loss, she studied sign language at the Rhode Island School for the Deaf. Her reading portfolio lists *The Jungle*, *A Brief History of Time*, *Schindler's List*, *Cry the Beloved Country*, and dozens of other books. For her senior project she helped to plan the Met's new health clinic, which included applying for and receiving a $10,000 planning grant and hiring a social worker to help with the project.

Julia's shyness has faded over time. Now she speaks with conviction, and her words reveal a dexterity with the higher-order thinking skills—analysis, evaluation, and application—that are the holy grail of modern education reform. "The Met treats you with more respect than other schools," Julia declares. "In my old schools, kids would get detentions if they didn't sit still or for calling a teacher by his first name. I just don't think that's right."

"So what happens *here* when people don't behave?" I ask.

"The *definition* of misbehaving is totally different here, which I think is good. I mean, it's borderline insanity to give someone a detention for chewing gum. And if you get in a fight here, you have to sit down with people and talk about it."

"I've always been an A student," she says, "but when I heard that the Met had no grades or honor roll, I didn't mind. Then last year I took a college course with grades, and it seemed funny that I was working so hard just for a letter, you know? That's when I kind of realized that in my old schools I'd gotten into this mentality that the letter was all that really mattered."

At the Met, Julia says, her motivation comes from doing interesting work and from her relationships with teachers and mentors. "I can talk to my advisor Emily about pretty much anything. She hassles me if I don't do my work, and that's annoying, but it's justified. She also helps me find resources and stuff like that. When I freaked out about my first biology test at Brown, she came over my house to help me study. Another time she brought me with her to a political protest."

Personalized learning carries over into Julia's learning team, which includes her teacher, parents, and LTI mentor. Even her grandparents occasionally drive from two states away to attend her exhibitions of what she has learned during the past quarter.

"Over time," Emily says, "Julia's learning team has realized that she needs to be on the verge of overload to feel really good about her work. Last semester we were afraid that we had pushed her too hard, so we suggested that she drop some things. She took our advice, but now she feels bad because she's not on the edge. So we're inviting her to bring back the intensity if that's what she wants."

"Julia is also very passionate about social issues," Emily continues, "so when we have classroom debates she gets indignant and says 'I can't believe you just said that!' Then she comes out with good facts to support her position, because she does a tremendous amount of reading. Sometimes she keeps quiet, because she doesn't want to seem like Miss Smarty Pants, but one of my pet peeves is when people downplay their intelligence—especially women. So we've talked about it and now Julia speaks more freely."

"Julia succeeded at the Met," I said to Emily, "but wouldn't she have succeeded at her hometown high school too? Why would a parent choose a school like the Met over a top-ranked suburban high school?"

"Working on liver cancer research at age 15 is more valuable than getting an A in any honors biology class," Emily responded. "Julia was working with real DNA, not looking at a double helix on a blackboard. Most high school biology is so oversimplified that it's not even really true. You memorize a sound bite for the test, but it doesn't mean much in the real world. Then you graduate and want to become a scientist, but you probably don't have the skills to reason through an original problem. Even kids like me who did science honors programs in high school, it was on a smaller scale, maybe for a month during the summer, and without the close, personal connections to adult scientists that Julia developed at her LTIs."

"Somebody said that Julia would have done great anywhere," Dennis added, "and that's only partially true. She would have been an A student at any school, absolutely. But she would have finished her work in 10 minutes and then gone off alone to read. At the Met she's done great academically but also became well-rounded socially. Some students would outscore her on the AP biology exams, but if you sat her down with biologists and asked them which student had the deepest *understanding* of the subject matter, Julia would win hands down."

"Originally the Met seemed like a pipe dream," says Julia's father, "and I was afraid to jeopardize her future. I was concerned about the lack of structure and how she'd get a good science and math background for college. But I've been very satisfied, and the colleges that accepted her were too. My hopes have been more than fulfilled."

Two Feet Ahead of the Train: Cesar's Story

> *Didn't hear the whistle*
> *Train's on the trestle*
> *I'm running for my life*
> *I'm too young to die*
> *Caught in the middle*
> *Train's big and I'm little*
> *And I'm two feet ahead of the train.*
> —Michael McNevin

Cesar arrived at the Met with a D+ average and sixth-grade skills in math and reading. His gang activities were escalating, and his father and brother were in prison. In a city where nearly half the Latino males drop out of high school, few people outside the Met expected him to graduate.

Summer is high season for gangs, so the Met helped Cesar arrange summer internships to keep him far away from Providence—Outward Bound in Utah, house building in Honduras, working at a summer camp in Pennsylvania. The wisdom of this strategy was tragically proven one summer when two of Cesar's close friends were murdered and several others were sent to the adult prison.

"They got charged with three life sentences and they're only 17," Cesar chokes up. "Now they're on their knees in some prison cell getting butt raped. I hate thinking about it, man. I'm a sensitive guy, and it makes we want to cry. If I'd been in a regular high school, I'd be in jail now too. I woulda had no future, and that's a fact. The Met teachers worry about you and take care of you, and they got me outa here for the summer, which is exactly what I needed."

"When I got to the Met I hated reading, I hated writing, I hated all of that. Then my teacher Hal showed me this book about the Ebola virus, *The Hot Zone*, by Richard Preston. He guaranteed I'd like it. So I said 'This is 500 pages, man—I can't read this!' Next thing I know I'm on page 32 and I'm yelling 'Hal, man, look at *this* part!' So I did a project on the Ebola virus, and I loved it. Best thing I ever did. I was talking just like a scientist, and Hal and my mom were really proud of my work. I thought maybe I'd really *become* a scientist someday. That project is why I stuck with the Met. Until then I was really doubting myself."

Before *The Hot Zone*, Cesar had never read a full-length book or written a paper. Now he writes to relieve stress and understand problems. "Last year I thought poetry was for wimps," he wrote in 10th grade, "but it's nothing like that—it's for people with feelings." Indeed, Cesar's feelings fill his brimming poetry notebooks:

> I was inches away from being a father.
> I wanted to say sorry for ruining your life,
> But happy because my first love was going to be my wife.
> The mother of my child, the father of her kid
> I was so happy and my soul was rich.
> I was gonna buy little blue outfits
> And father-and-son matching suits,
> But I didn't want to know what it was until it was due.
>
> But my first love had lied, just to see what I would say.
> At that moment a part in my head was dead.

I felt an emptiness and anger, and I have never forgave her.
Maybe this will teach me to be careful who I choose.
And it might be selfish, but I didn't use protection on purpose.
She didn't want me to wear one either, so I found them useless.
I wonder if she realizes how much that little lie affected me.
For the rest of the year I was left heart broken and lonely.

"I figured out that writing isn't as hard as I always thought," Cesar says. "Now I always carry around a notebook to write in. I've got to, man. So many ideas come into my mind when I'm walking or on the bus. I got the idea of carrying a note pad from a rapper named DMX."

Now Cesar is slated to be assistant director of the General Reading Center at the special-needs camp where he was a counselor last summer. "I love reading and writing," Cesar says, "so I wanted to work at the GRC. They hired me because last summer the kids would be rapping, and I'd say 'Why don't you write your own raps, man?' They said they didn't know how, so I'm pulling out my big notebook and showing them. They're looking at my stuff and saying to each other 'Hey man, read this yo! Read this!' So I taught them how to write raps during bunk hours."

"The Met is one of the best schools to improve on these skills," Cesar says. "At other schools the teacher is up front telling you where put commas, so you zone out, talk to the guy next to you, lean back in your chair, write some bull crap, and draw pictures on the back. Here at the Met you write about what you're interested in, so you really *want* to write. You also get more mature. You learn to say to yourself 'No, I can't talk to my friends right now. I need to put myself in a quiet room, write in my journal, write my proposal, all of that.'"

Unlike Cesar's communication skills, his math and science progress at the Met was limited. He learned arithmetic—a big step forward—but little algebra or other advanced math. His most ambitious plan was to do budget projections for the small retail store where he was doing an LTI, but the owner changed his mind and hired an accountant instead.

Cesar matured over time, but he struggled with poor work habits. Several times he came close to dropping out, and early in 11th grade he started a fight with another student. "I had just spent the summer in Honduras, and I was so proud of the hard work we did building houses for poor people. Then I came back to Providence, and suddenly I was being hard core on the streets again. One time I got thrown from a moving car and slammed against the pavement and almost got my head ran over. Another time I fought three guys in their 30s and I got beat up really bad. It makes you feel like you're nothing.

"So when I came into 11th grade at the Met, I was at the point where I didn't care if I lived or died. Then I heard that Derek was talkin' junk about me. He was sayin' he'd fight me anytime I wanted. So the next day at school everyone was standin' around and I walked up to him with my arms wide open and I'm like 'Derek, Derek, Derek.'

"So he's like 'You got somethin' to say to me, man?'

"And I said 'I heard you was talkin' junk about me, man.'

"So he dropped his bag, which is like 'What's up? Let's do this.'

"And I just hit him. Boom. And I heard the smack. Smack. Everybody was shocked."

"We told Cesar he'd have to leave if it happened again," his advisor Hal says. "We suspended him for 2 weeks while we looked for ways to get him off the street for a while, but we were in touch with him and his family the whole time. Cesar had just seen a couple of people get shot in his neighborhood, and I think the fight was a way of spilling out the pain."

"When I came back from being suspended," Cesar says, "a lot of teachers started talking to me. And they got a lot of the other kids in my advisory to talk to me too. All these people were saying how they're worried about me, and it made me start worrying about myself, you know what I mean? It was like 'Man, where am I? What am I doing? I was such a good student. What happened?'"

Cesar's mother remembers the Met's compassion after the fight. "Hal and Elliot came over the house, and they weren't sure if Cesar would be able to stay at the Met. But I was desperate for him to stay in school. Thank God they understood all the pressure and anger my son was feeling. After they left I was so grateful, and I sat down with Cesar, and we were crying, and tears were coming down, and I told him 'This isn't what I want for you. Please

understand this is not what I want. I want the best for you. I want
you in high school.'"

Most schools are quick to expel students like Cesar, but the
Met was determined to keep him in school. They arranged for him
to finish 11th grade at a residential school in Minnesota for at-risk
students. After that they would decide if he could come back. But
he never gave the new program a chance; he returned to Providence
after just one week. The Met was upset to see their hard-won
solution unravel so quickly, but they also understood that Cesar
had returned, at least in part, to resume his role as protector and
father-figure for his two younger sisters. The Met continued pushing him to commit to his schoolwork.

"Hal told me I couldn't stay at the Met if I didn't do my work,"
Cesar says. "So I did it, and I'm still doing it. One day Hal wrote
in my journal 'Seeing you so excited about learning is a high point
in my days.' That made me feel really good, you know what I
mean?

"When I was in Minnesota, I was reading *The Autobiography
of Malcolm X*, which Hal gave as a going-away present. Malcolm
is my idol, because he had the courage to speak out. He moved
up from his hustling life and prison and used his angry attitude
positively, you know what I mean? So I was like 'I'm going back
to the Met, and I'm gonna change. I'm gonna do my work, and I
ain't gonna play around no more. Colleges look at your last 2 years,
so it's time to get busy.'"

This is a student who barely passed eighth grade. Now he's
drawing moral lessons from a classic autobiography. He's lingering
after school in search of the perfect words for his poetry. And he
has accepted a scholarship from a small private college near Boston.
To succeed there he will need reliable supports and better work
habits, but the remarkable fact is that he stayed in high school
and traded instant wealth on the streets for the faint promise of
education's long-term rewards.

Faced with a similar trade-off decades earlier, young Malcolm
X chose the street. When he said he wanted to become a lawyer,
his favorite teacher told him to select a more realistic "nigger profession" like carpentry. Malcolm left school, and for many years his
mentors were mostly hustlers and inmates. With the right encour-

agement at school, perhaps he could have achieved his greatness without the intervening years of crime and punishment.

"All the friends I've lost," Cesar says, "that was God giving me a slap on the neck. I've had so many chances to push some serious heroin and get rich. But not me, man. I got lucky to be in the right place at the right time. I could have gone down, but I'm headed up instead. You see, I'm GHETTO—Getting Higher Education To Teach Others. That's what ghetto means to me. I'm a leader, but the thing is that I don't want people to follow me. I want them to lead too, you know what I mean?"

2 Personalized Learning

Maybe nothing is intrinsically interesting. Knowledge gains its meaning, at least initially, through a touch on the shoulder, through a conversation. . . . My first enthusiasm about writing came because I wanted a teacher to like me.

—Mike Rose, *Lives on the Boundary*

The Power of Smallness

Pink Floyd's movie *The Wall* depicts schools as conveyor belts that dump students into monstrous machines and spew them out as ground meat. "All in all we're just another brick in the wall," shout the students, condemning schools that worship industrial efficiency but ignore human needs. Many reformers now reject the prevailing factory model of education, insisting that schools aren't assembly lines and that learning happens best when tailored to each student's needs.

"One student at a time" is the Met's mantra, and the school acts on it with remarkable consistency. Their first step is creating small schools and small classrooms. Currently they have two schools, each with 110 students, eight teachers, a director, a workplace coordinator, and other administrative and specialty staff. One school is located on the fourth floor of a downtown office building, and the other is two miles away in a new school building. The Met's campus is still under construction, scheduled to open in 2002. It will have six small school buildings, each for about 110 students, plus a shared building with a library, auditorium, gymnasium, health clinic, multimedia studio, cafeteria, and other facilities.

A primary goal of Met teachers is knowing all of their students well. Most high schools make this impossible by assigning more than 100 students to every teacher. With responsibility for more than 20 students during each class period, no teacher can provide much individual attention. Nor can they comment adequately on assignments, because spending even 10 minutes per student each week would require 20 hours of work after school. That's on top of lesson planning, lunch duty, study halls, office hours, staff meetings, and advising student activities.

The Met also insists on the value of small schools. The average size of American schools has increased sixfold since 1950, and by 1986 half of all high schools had more than 1,000 students (Tyack & Cuban, 1995). Conventional wisdom says that large high schools cost less, offer more courses, and win more trophies. But these beliefs deserve a closer look, particularly after a federally funded review of 103 studies found "small schools to be superior to large schools on most measures and equal on the rest" (Cotton, 1996, p. 2).

The extra courses offered by large high schools are often targeted to the most advanced students (Haller, Monk, Spotted Bear, Griffith, & Moss, 1990). Less advanced students are placed in less demanding classrooms, which widens an achievement gap that often parallels racial and economic lines (Lee & Smith, 1994). For many parents the bottom line is college, and Cotton found that SAT scores and college-acceptance rates of small schools are equal or superior to those of large schools.

The "economies of scale" argument—that large schools cost less per student—has driven increases in school size. But large schools also have *penalties* of scale, such as extra administrative and security costs (Klonsky, 1995). The principal of a large suburban high school told me that crime plummeted after he installed surveillance cameras in every hallway. But Deborah Meier argues that small schools "offer what metal detectors and guards cannot: the safety and security of being where you are known well by people who care for you" (1995, p. 112). She reports that small, alternative schools in New York City have lower levels of theft and violence than other schools, even though they often serve the most difficult students. At the Met, 80% of parents strongly agree that "this school is a safe place," compared with 33% of high school parents statewide (Rhode Island Department of Education, 1999).

Small schools have higher graduation rates (Cotton, 1996), which reduces the total cost per graduate (Stiefel, Berne, Iatarola, & Fruchter, 2000). It also saves public costs in the long run, because each completed year of high school reduces by 35% the likelihood that an individual will later become dependent on public welfare (Carnegie Council on Adolescent Development, 1989). Carnegie also reports that each year's class of dropouts will cost the nation about $260 billion in lost earnings and taxes during their lifetimes. Keeping students in school is a wise investment, and cost per graduate, a statistic that is rarely discussed, may be more important than cost per student.

As for more trophies, who could argue? Met students may never have the thrill of winning state championships, but their small school leagues provide most of the same benefits (and drawbacks) of taking part in competitive sports, debate, and other teams. Cotton's (1996) review found that small schools offer fewer activities overall but have more opportunities *per student* and higher rates of participation. Students in small schools also participate in a wider range of activities, take on more responsibility, and enjoy their participation more than students in large schools (Barker & Gump, 1964; Cotton, 1996).

One challenge of small schools is finding enough staff to supervise after-school activities. "That was easier at my last school, because it was bigger," Dennis says. "I'd always have 9 or 10 teachers at basketball games, another group who liked tutoring students after school, and another group that loved dances. At the Met I have to be careful about how many teachers I assign to each activity. Coverage will be easier once we've finished building our six small schools and have more staff."

Effective schools need intensive discussions among staff, says Deborah Meier (1995), and making that happen is easier when the staff is small enough to meet around a single table. Smallness also allows teachers to know each other well enough to provide well-informed support and suggestions to each other, and to feel and act collectively responsible for each student's success.

It's not practical to replace large buildings with small ones, but many schools have adopted "school-within-a-school" designs that bring small-school advantages to large buildings. One huge Manhattan high school split into four small schools, a Head Start program, a teen parenting program, and a teacher training center (Cushman, 1997). Dennis believes that school-within-a-school de- signs should have multiple schools in a single building, not a single school with multiple subdivisions. He says that the latter often leads to elitism and resentment, because one group ends up being seen as having special status or privileges that are unfair to the other groups. (Donna Muncey and Patrick McQuillan document this problem in their 1996 book about the Coalition of Essential Schools.)

The Met's new campus will have four small schools plus the shared facility (described above) on one plot of land, and then two more small schools several blocks away. Constructing the six schools as separate buildings is intended to enhance the benefits of smallness and to avoid any pressures that might arise in the future for the Met to become a single, larger school.

One of the new schools has already been built, and its design reflects the Met's personalized and project-oriented approach to learning. Walking at an unhurried pace, students can traverse the school's two farthest points in about 40 seconds. It's about the size of five tennis courts (13,000 square feet) and from the outside looks more like a community center than a school. In the center is a very large, high-ceilinged room used for whole-school events, student projects, eating lunch, and many other functions. At each corner of that hub is a cluster of four rooms that contain individual and small-group work spaces, computers, telephones, couches, and teachers' offices. The rest of the school, also surrounding the main room, consists of an administrative area, a conference room, a performance room, a kitchen, and a quiet study room with a small library. Outside is half an acre of lawns, terraces, gardens, and parking areas, plus two immense murals designed by students and painted onto the walls of adjacent buildings.

Relationships and Respect

Schools do not become personalized simply by getting smaller, and reducing class size has little impact if everything else stays the same (Murnane & Levy, 1996a). But the Met has done far more than just reduce class size. Students are divided into groups of 14, known as an "advisory," which replaces the traditional classroom. A primary teacher or "advisor" oversees their learning and generally stays with them for all 4 years of high school. The advisory is designed to be a small, supportive group of learners and an extended family in which all students feel well known both personally and academically.

Advisories meet for an hour in the morning and a half-hour in the afternoon. In the morning, while students recount their latest knee surgery or weekend road trip, they take out their daily planners and schedule the day's activities. Then they work through a math problem together, plan a museum trip, write a letter to the editor, or discuss homelessness. Once or twice a year they take outdoor trips together to build group spirit.

Advisors touch base daily with every student and schedule frequent one-on-one meetings. They become deeply familiar with each student's abilities, needs, and interests so that they can suggest well-informed strategies for each student's learning. Advisors also come to know their students' families through frequent phone calls, school events, committee meetings, and quarterly exhibitions and learning-team meetings where parents help to assess their child's progress and plan their curriculum. Later chapters discuss all of these activities in more detail.

Many parents find it helpful to have the advisor as a single contact person. "Jamar had seven or eight teachers in junior high," one mother says, "and it was impossible to reach all of them. We couldn't even find out what we needed to do to help him. The guidance counselor came up with a form that each teacher had to fill out every week with Jamar's assignments, but when any single layer broke down, the whole thing broke down. At the Met there's one central person who knows Jamar's strengths and weaknesses across all subjects, and I can reach her easily whenever I want to."

The advisory system ensures that someone will always be there to help students work out problems. In most schools that is the role of guidance counselors, but they are usually responsible for hundreds of students. The Met believes that the trusting, day-to-day relationship that develops between a student and a caring advisor will lead to better solutions when problems arise. Advisors often serve as confidants, coaches, sounding boards, and intermediaries.

Recently in a suburban classroom outside Boston, a first grader mentioned out of the blue that her mother was dead. The teacher notified the guidance counselor, but neither adult inquired further before the end of the school day. The girl went home to where her diabetic mother had died that morning. After doing homework and eating leftovers, the girl spent the night sleeping in her dead mother's arms. "This is a story for our time," commented Diane Levin, a professor of early childhood education. "As we're under more and more pressure to focus on things like [state achievement tests], there's less and less focus on the well-being of our kids. Teachers are being forced to short-change the stuff that's really best for the children" (in Bombardieri, 1999).

Large classrooms and impersonal schools make such tragedies inevitable. The incident underscores the Met's bedrock stance that academic and personal matters are closely intertwined. One morning I sat in Adam's advisory while a circle of 10 students discussed current events. At break time Adam approached the girl sitting across from me and asked what was wrong. She started crying and said that her close friend had been missing for 2 days. Until Adam acted, I had no inkling that anything was amiss. He noticed because he knew her well. After he took her aside to listen and discuss next steps, she was calm enough to rejoin the discussion. A teacher who lacked the time, inclination, or skill to intervene would have overlooked a powerful obstacle to her learning.

Even if a teacher wants to intervene, many schools frown on it. In my teacher certification program, one professor told us: "You need to go in there as a taskmaster and get a pound of flesh from these kids. None of this Mr. Big Heart stuff! Do your job and then close your door. If you want to get involved personally with students, look into becoming a guidance counselor." Another instructor said, "Don't smile at the students until Thanksgiving."

Mr. Big Heart is alive and well at the Met, and intense relationships often develop between students and advisors. Tamika and her advisor, Marcus, sometimes refer to each other as brother and sister. "I see what Tamika has and doesn't have in her life," Marcus says, "and sometimes I put myself out there perhaps more than I should. But then who's to say how much I should? She doesn't have an older brother, she doesn't live with her father, and I just got caught up in the relationship in an ultra-positive way, because

I want to help her the *best* way I can and in *any* way I can." Many educators would say that Marcus has "bad boundaries," but the Met takes the opposite view.

When I asked Tamika if she keeps in touch with the school over the summer, she responded that teachers write her letters and that she can call them if she wants. Those facts alone speak volumes about the school. But then I asked if she had ever had a *reason* to call over the summer. She looked puzzled, so I rephrased my question slightly. She still looked puzzled but finally said, "Yeah, I've called over the summer. Just to say hi and everything, you know?" That's when I realized why my question was confusing. It was as if I had asked "Have you ever had a reason to call your *family* over the summer?" Most people don't need a reason to call their family. They're part of your life and you want to be in touch. It was the same for Tamika and the Met.

"I like the Met because you have a close relationship with your teacher," said another student. "It's not like a regular school where I'm confused but I don't say nothing 'cause I don't like my teacher. I procrastinate a lot, and when I had to write this essay for an Outward Bound scholarship, my teacher was like 'You're *not* putting this one off. It's too important. You're coming over my house, and you're writing it.' And I stayed at her house until eight o'clock that night and got it done. Then when I got the scholarship she took me shopping and paid for my boots, because my mother didn't have the money. My mother paid her back later. Stuff like that. Like I used to have a big, big attitude about adults trying to have authority over me. I'm getting better, but last year she was the only one who could calm me down and get me to go apologize. She knows how I am, and if she knows that I'm *too* upset then she'll just leave me alone and let me work by myself."

This student's final words make it clear that there are times when students *don't* want to be close with their advisors. "Understanding the student is great," Dennis says, "but you don't want to go overboard. Sometimes a student says 'Get out of my face. That's my life you're poking into, and this is school.' We try to respect that, although we often tell students that their life both inside *and* outside of school is our concern."

The Met is a web of relationships. "Everyone in my advisory has this amazing bond with each other," Cesar says. "When you

stick together for 4 years you gain lifelong friends. We can talk to
our advisor Hal about anything, and he listens because he wants
to, not because he has to. I've also gained love and respect for Doc
[Dennis] and Elliot—they're like fathers to me. Anita [the office
manager] is like everybody's mother. I can't imagine the Met without the people it has in it. Everybody here is part of the community."

Parents and internship mentors complete this circle of intimacy. One night Milan's parents breezed into the Met with open
arms and kissed their son's advisor on both cheeks. Another student's mentor said "Pablo and I have a relationship now. He can
call me anytime if he needs something. That will always be true,
even after he leaves here."

Relationships develop between parents and mentors too. "I
love this child," said Carlita's mentor. "She's like my little girl. I'm
concerned about her future, so I made up my mind to get her into
a summer math program that would help her get into college. But
her parents weren't going to allow it, because they wanted her
help with their home business. They also want her to get into
college though, and I thought the math program would help with
that. I've met them a few times when I've dropped off Carlita at
home, and I feel bad that we can't speak the same language. They
know I love their daughter and have high expectations for her,
and they realize that I'm helping her succeed in this new culture.
They keep a very close rein on her, but they've let it go somewhat
with me because of the trust we've developed. In the end they
agreed to let her do the summer program."

The Met's focus on relationships has built a vital community
that makes the school stronger. One week the Met's parent newsletter said, "The families of two Met students are in crisis. If any
family would consider taking in these students, please call Jill or
Anita in the main office." Just one week later, the newsletter said,
"Our thanks go out to everyone who called about helping Met
students in crisis. Two families have each graciously taken in a
student, and they are facing the challenges with love and generosity.
It makes us so proud of our community."

Also typical was an incident from orientation week. Students
were introducing themselves during a group activity, and Simon
was feeling new and out of place. Apologetically, he described

himself as socially awkward. Another student asked, "What does socially awkward mean?"

"It means I don't have many friends and I'm not good at making them."

"Honey, that's not true," insisted an older student. "You're at the Met. Here we're all your friends."

To help create a warm and respectful school environment, Dennis and Elliot lead by example. To say that their doors are open would be an understatement; when they're away from their desks, students hold meetings in their offices and use their telephones. (The principal of my hometown elementary school cultivated such a fearsome image that 200 spirited children would instantly fall silent when he entered the cafeteria.) More than just knowing every student by name, Dennis and Elliot monitor their progress and often get deeply involved. They drive students home and have long talks while the car idles. They counsel students who come to them about pregnancies. They help irresolute parents to be more authoritative. And they push students to stay in school.

"I just tell students that they're *not* dropping out," Elliot says. "Dierdre's mom says 'Well, it's up to her. If she wants to leave, she can leave.' And I say 'No, she can't! If you talk like that, she'll think she can do anything she wants.' Her plan was to go down to Florida and hook up with some older guy or some crazy thing. She's 17 years old! So I told her 'You can't drop out. I won't sign the papers. You *think* you'll get a GED and go to college, but within 2 months you'll be pregnant and he'll dump you. Then no one will rent you an apartment and you'll be living on the street. So you're not leaving. You're just not leaving.' And it worked. She stayed. Sometimes you have to do something desperate like that. By delaying her for a few days, we bought her the time she needed to change her mind. Sometimes you have to be parental, because no one else is doing it."

As Dennis roams the school, he constantly expresses warmth and concern for students:

"How's your sister doing after her surgery?"

"Great job, man—I hear you got the scholarship!"

"Did you make that call to the mayor's office?"

Or just exchanging a raised-fist power symbol with a student at the far end of the hall. He carries colorful stones in his pocket and lends them to students who need support. "When you're about to explode at somebody," he told one girl, "grip the stone and think it through." The next day she returned the stone with a note saying, "Dear Doc, thank you for lending me the stone yesterday. I'm cured now. I know what to do when I get mad, so you can have it back."

"Personalization isn't about being best buddies," Dennis says. "It's about respect and listening and treating people well. I've told some of my toughest students to be here at 4:00 P.M., to sit down and we were going to look at some book together. And they came, because we had a relationship. Or you have Lisa, who just learned to multiply last week at age 16. Now she's saying she likes math and wants to learn more. And it's because she likes her teachers and they respect her and listen to her voice. For many students, that's what makes them relax and want to learn."

When one of Isaac's students had an operation, he visited her at the hospital every day for 2 weeks, including several hours on the weekend. The parents weren't there much of the time, so Isaac was playing a needed role, but wasn't he overstepping some boundaries? Not in the Met's opinion. Isaac insisted that a 14-year-old shouldn't be left alone in a hospital without an advocate. She had been wetting her bed because the nurses were too overloaded to help her in time, and once when Isaac walked in she was alone, crying in pain after a spinal tap.

"I think it's great that Isaac is visiting her," Dennis says. "If he feels *obligated* to spend so much time there, then he's wrong. If he's resenting it, then it's too much. But if he's got the time and feels that she needs it right now, then I support that. I believe that the more time you give people the better. The boundaries totally depend on the situation and how much time you have. The bottom line is that Isaac is developing a bond with her at a crucial time in her life, and that bond will help him work with her for the next 4 years."

The Met is not trying to undermine or replace parents; in fact, the school makes great efforts to work closely with parents. But the staff see themselves as raising children too, so they go beyond the usual boundaries.

There are boundaries, however. "There was one student I had *huge* problems with," an advisor says. "I tried my hardest and did a million things to help, but he pushed things too far. In all honesty, there really wasn't much I liked about him. He constantly lied and stole and broke the rules. He would deal drugs at school, and he was so cocky and arrogant about everything. He pushed all my buttons. Once he even told me to fuck off, and I kicked him out of the advisory until he gave me a sincere apology the next week. But I still kept trying and trying. His main goal in life was to be a music executive with fancy cars and all that, which really turns me off, but I kept encouraging him and saying 'If that's what you really want, then here are the things you have to do.' After a ton of legwork, I found him this amazing internship with the production manager of a large recording studio, but he didn't do his work and had to leave. And he never stopped lying and being rude and arrogant.

"At some point I said to him, 'You've used up everything I had inside me to give you. I don't have anything left. If you want to stay here, it's all up to you now. I can't think of anything else to do. And to be honest, I'm not *willing* to put in any more because you've thrown it back in my face too many times. It's your life, so you take it and succeed or fail.' And a week later he left the Met. It was really sad, but I waited until it was totally unworkable. I got advice from everyone about other things to try, but nothing helped. For my own health and sanity, and for the benefit of the other students in my advisory, we decided it was time to end things.

"His story has an amazing addendum, though. Dennis always says that you never know what students will take away with them. They don't seem to be hearing you at all, but then something you did will come back and help them years later. Well, over the summer I got a phone message from this same student. I thought maybe he needed something, so I called him back and said 'Hey, what are you doing?'

"'I just called to wish you a happy birthday!' he said.

"'I can't believe you remembered my birthday!'

"'Well, you *were* my teacher! And I just wanted to call and say that I miss you guys at the Met.'

"'That's so nice!' I said, and we chatted for a couple minutes. So who knows? I guess we touched him in some way. Why else would he call? Last week he called again. He's failing out of his new school and talked about coming back to the Met, but I don't think it's going to work out."

Even in more run-of-the-mill situations, personalized learning has its boundaries. One student has adopted a spot in the main office where she spends hours reading books and absorbing adult conversations. Sitting on the carpet just outside Dennis's office door, she tarnishes the orderly image that many administrators cherish. But rather than bristling at her lack of decorum, Dennis welcomed her by taping her photograph onto the wall just above where she sits. The Met has its own rules of decorum, however. One day she curled up asleep in the warm sun, and Dennis didn't hesitate to wake her and say that sleeping there was unacceptable. He was good-humored about it—not angry or punitive—but the boundaries were clear.

Many of the problems facing modern education are beyond the Met's control, and the Met's personalized approach raises some problems that other schools avoid. Some students arrive tired and undernourished, with attention spans no longer than a music video, from dangerous neighborhoods or houses without books. Other students want no part of the Met's intimacy. "At my old school the teachers didn't mess with the tough kids like me," one student says. "They mostly paid attention to the motivated kids. Here at the Met the teachers give everyone a lot of attention—sometimes a little *too* much attention. My advisor is always on top of me."

Staying on top of students requires stamina. Advisors and students stay together for 4 years, so advisors can't write off a difficult student by saying "I can hang on until June." Students have occasionally been assigned to a different advisor in response to irreconcilable problems, but only after the advisor had gone to great lengths in search of solutions. In schools where teachers have more than 100 students, it's not possible to have time-consuming personal investments in more than a fraction of them. Difficult students slip through the cracks with minimal friction, and many dedicated teachers get worn down and demoralized by the impossibility of meeting their students' needs.

An opposite dynamic plays out at the Met. Students never slip unnoticed through the cracks, because each advisor has primary responsibility for only 14 students. When students fail, it's wrenching for advisors who have invested deeply in the student and tried everything without success. But all of that effort does make the failure a little easier to accept.

"When one of my students fails," an advisor says, "it feels so different than at my old school where I had 120 students. In the end, I know that I've done so much to support them. At my old school, I didn't even really know who they *were*. I just knew they were hurting. I didn't know them well enough to ask why, and I didn't have a relationship with their parents. I couldn't get to the bottom of anything. All I knew is that they were kids in pain who were really isolated and really hated school for whatever reason."

Despite the challenges, the advisors I've spoken with love their jobs. Those who have taught at other schools say the Met's lows are lower and the highs are higher. "It's a real privilege to be allowed the kind of access to the lives of these young people that the structure of the Met creates," one advisor says. "There is the real potential for me to impact both the learning *and* the life of *every* student in my advisory. My friends who teach in other schools tell me that they just don't feel that way."

Prospects for Personalized Schools

Personalized education has become more mainstream in recent years. The 1996 *Breaking Ranks* report by two of America's leading education policy groups—the National Association of Secondary School Principals and the Carnegie Foundation for the Advancement of Teaching—calls for large high schools to break into units of no more than 600 students, with each teacher responsible for no more than 90 students. (By Met standards, these numbers are a step in the right direction but still too large.) The report urges schools to create custom learning plans and designate "personal adult advocates" for every student. It urges teachers to vary their instructional strategies in ways that engage student interests and accommodate individual learning styles.

Four years later, the U.S. Department of Education launched the Class-Size Reduction Program, pledging $12.4 billion over 7 years to help schools hire 100,000 new teachers and thereby reduce class size and increase personal attention. The Smaller Learning Communities Initiative pledged another $45 million to help large high schools partition themselves into smaller learning communities of no more than 600 students in order "to create a more personalized high school experience" (U.S. Department of Education, 2000). Private foundations are also funding personalized education, such as a recent $30 million grant from the Carnegie Foundation, Gates Foundation, and Open Society Institute to reorganize 10 of New York City's largest and lowest-performing high schools into dozens of smaller high schools with fewer than 500 students each (Lewis, 2001).

Although these ideas have entered the mainstream, their implementation lags far behind. Many districts lack the political will needed to make significant changes, and other districts have the will but don't know what steps to take. Understanding the Met is important, because it provides a working example for educators, parents, and policymakers who are trying to make education more personalized.

3 Learning Through Interests

"When you ask people about their best learning experiences," Dennis says, "it was when something was important to them, when it had meaning for them. Research shows the same thing. Like a few years back when I wanted to build a greenhouse, I took a botany course, read books, talked to experts, and soaked in everything.

"Students always ask, 'When will I ever use this?' They can't see how school connects to their future, and that saps their motivation. When you work hard on something in the real world, it's usually because you see how it connects to your goals. Students learn better when school makes those connections clear. That's why you have to know each student as an individual. Then you can make the connections between what already interests them and what they need to learn.

"Take the war right now in Kosovo. We can discuss that war and the major wars in history, but it works better if we start by connecting it to the student's life. One student told me, 'I just try to survive every night. I ride around in the car with my boys, and I hope to make it through the night alive.' That's where the real war is for some of our students. Other students know about conflicts from fighting with their siblings or parents. So we can use that as a jumping-off point to understand other wars, other historical events, other social phenomena.

"Or take Jamar, for example. He's brilliant, but he had a horrible time up through middle school. He was so quiet and shy when he arrived here that you could barely hear his voice. Then we helped him develop his passion for computers. Suddenly he was taking a physics class, designing a computer game, reading a book about the history of the world, studying on weekends, and doing an internship at a computer company. One day something went wrong with the company's software, and they had to come pick him up at school because he was the only one who knew how to fix it. In the meantime he's studied calculus, learned three computer languages, written a software manual, and spent a year studying in Japan.

"So what got Jamar to blossom? It was having people who respected him, treated him well, and allowed him to follow his passions. Our approach is challenging, because we have to find something different for every student. It's hard to help some students figure out their interests, or to get them engaged once they've figured out their interests. But it's worth the challenge, because following interests is how people learn best."

In his book *Interests of Mind* (in progress), Arthur Powell points out that few students are deeply interested in their studies, and that students who *do* show strong interests are often derided by their peers. He offers the following two scenarios. First, a few 10th graders in the cafeteria are arguing loudly about the causes of the Civil War. "Why are you talking about that *here*?" sneers a student at an adjacent table. "Don't you know we're not in class anymore?" Second, some 12th graders have just completed their Advanced Placement chemistry exam after a year of demanding preparation. "Thank goodness it's over!" one of them says, exiting the exam room. "Just think—never again in our whole lives will we have to spend another *second* thinking about chemistry." The others nod their heads in agreement.

In contrast, Cesar was still excited about his Ebola virus project 3 years after completing it. "I loved that project," he says. "My boys told me to shut up about it, but I was too excited. The top scientists in the world have these meetings once a year, and they talk about viruses. I wanted to *be* at one of them meetings—in India or Switzerland or wherever—because I had learned so much. I knew I could of sat down and had a really good conversation with them, you know what I mean? I knew so many statistics—I mean stats, whatever you call it—and I *loved* it."

"Students whose curiosity ends at the classroom door are not considered a national problem," Powell (in progress) says. But he argues that most students "lack focus, direction, and passion. They seem burned out, or perhaps were never lit up. They go through the academic motions with perfunctory competence, but they lack sustaining interests."

Overcoming that problem is one of the Met's fundamental goals. The school devotes much of its energy to helping students grasp the pleasurable and life-enhancing aspects of learning. At most schools, high grades and test scores are the pinnacle of achievement. But the Met's pinnacle is becoming a passionate, lifelong learner, and the school believes that using interests as the starting point for learning is the best way to achieve that goal.

When students in most schools are allowed to pursue their interests—selecting their own essay topic, for example—it's usually within rigid guidelines. "A student can have a personal style or a consuming interest," says Ted Sizer, "as long as it fits into the usual pattern of subjects that are taught largely in isolation from each other. But there is precious little room for the student who might harbor interests not reflected by a particular school's division of faculty labor. . . . Unless an aggressive student or his or her parents or an influential teacher pushes for an exception, nothing happens. There is little incentive for intellectual or social idiosyncrasy" (1999, p. 8).

My own education bears this out. During high school I was on a Native American dance team, and in 10th-grade English class I wrote a term paper about it and danced for my classmates in full regalia. It's one of my few high school papers that escaped the recycling bin. "Because you are so interested in ceremony and ritual," the teacher wrote, "you might be interested in reading and studying the psychological and symbolic significance of ritual universally. Your report could lead into an interesting project on the difference between folk art and formal art."

His suggestions were terrific, but I didn't follow through. Perhaps I was lazy, but it wouldn't have hurt if he had offered to excuse me from other class requirements if I decided to follow his suggestions. Then pursuing my interests would have been an integral part of the curriculum rather than an addition to an already demanding workload.

Pursuing interests was even discouraged at times in my doctoral program, despite the importance of each student developing a professional niche. In one course we had to write a paper on a major childhood transition relevant to psychotherapy. The professor not only rejected my request to write about adoption—a strong interest of mine—but was visibly annoyed that I hadn't chosen any of the topics that *he* had proposed. With a huff that made me wonder about his own childhood transitions, he made the absurd claim that adoption wasn't relevant enough to psychotherapy. So instead of adoption, I selected puberty for my magnum oedipus—I mean opus.

If interest-based learning is to flourish, educators will have to weave it into the core structure of the school, rather than expecting its impetus to come from students. The Met emphasizes interests from the beginning. "With Stefano it was easy," his advisor says, "because he arrived with a passion he already wanted to pursue. He wanted to be an animal biologist, so he did his first internship at the zoo. His main project was researching some new animals for the zoo to acquire, figuring out what habitats they would need and all that. Some of my other students have arrived with so many interests that they try to take on more projects than they can handle. Then my job is to help them make choices or pursue different interests across the four years of high school."

But most students are less sure of their interests. Few have given the question much thought, or else they haven't thought much beyond television, fashion, and popular music. Not that those are invalid interests—in fact, students have completed valuable projects in all of those areas. But many students have not been exposed to a vast number of other topics that they might also find interesting.

Another issue arises with students whose interests have been imposed from the outside. Alfie Kohn (1998a) talks about parents who anxiously dictate all of their child's activities with an eye toward someday impressing a Harvard admissions committee—a process Kohn calls "preparation H." He argues that these children gradually lose sight of what they personally enjoy and find interesting.

The Met has designed many activities to help students identify their interests. Advisories take trips to museums, court hearings, organic farms, and air traffic control towers. Morning assemblies often feature guests who talk about their jobs and interests, and the Met has an annual event at which parents do the same. Students are encouraged to interview and observe people whose work interests them, and parents are asked to recall what topics and activities have engaged their child's interest over the years. Students also do interest-exploration activities such as the following:

- Past Life Journey Map: Create a map of your important life experiences—people, hobbies, special talents, group activities, music, books, movies, beliefs about society, jobs, good times, hard times, things from your culture (art, language, traditions, rituals, religion), and anything else that has shaped the way you think and act.
- Future Life Journey Map: What do you want your life to look like 2, 5, 10, and 25 years from now? Include employment, education, hobbies, skills, travel, spirituality, character, and location. Imagine your retirement party. You have accomplished your most important life goals. Who is there, and what are they saying about you as a person? What are they saying about the events of your life?
- What are the greatest sources of suffering in the world? In your country? In your community? What are the most critical needs that are going unmet? Which businesses, organizations, or individuals are involved in solving these problems?
- See a play or movie that interests you and explore it in depth: Read the history of the period. Why were the clothes like that? Compare the language from then to now. Read a biography of the main character. Dig deeper into anything that grabs your interest.
- Talk with more experienced students about their passions. How did they figure out what they like to do? Do the same thing with parents, relatives, neighbors, church members, and retired adults.
- Other activities: Scavenger hunt, skill inventory, career interest checklist, library and Internet search, oral history of someone who interests you, autobiographical sketch, family history.

"Most students eventually identify interests, but not all," Dennis says. "We just can't find something that Terry loves. He's a junior, but he's not doing *anything*. We can't figure out what to do with him. So we're taking a much more directive stance, even though we don't like doing that. We placed him at Global Harvest working on hunger issues, and he writes a lot so we hooked him up for an hour a day with an advisor who likes writing. I told him, 'We can't have you just hanging out all the time waiting for the perfect internship to come along. So feel free to find something you like better, but in the meantime you need to do these things we've assigned.'"

Students can't be idle just because they can't identify any interests. Nor can they disregard an important skill just because they find it boring. "Learning through interests doesn't mean you can do whatever you want," Elliot says. "You can *start* anywhere you want, but then you need to take it to an intellectual level. One student said he was going to watch TV all day because that was his interest. But that's not how it works. We want to help students find joy in learning and become useful citizens. To do that you need to learn how to use your mind well. Through your interests you need to learn how to reason effectively and grapple with what you're learning."

"Many things you love also have parts you hate," an advisor adds. "Students need to learn that. Jake wants to be a marine biologist, but he's disorganized and hates writing. His internship mentors convinced him that he needs to overcome those barriers to become a scientist, so he wrote a 15-page research paper on the winter flounder. His mentors needed the information for their work. Jake hated every second of it, but he did it. After a dozen drafts he ended up with an amazing, college-level paper. If you get students hooked on their interests, sometimes they're willing to do the less appealing parts. Sometimes they even end up *enjoying* those parts."

And other times they don't. "We're very flexible with Tony," Dennis says, "but our idea of school will never match what he wants. He already has the skills to run his own business, but I know that he's never going to do much homework. Some people would kick him out for that, but I wouldn't. He's a great kid, and he's not hurting anyone. If we're patient and resourceful, then maybe we'll get him excited about learning, and that will help him for the next 60 years. That's what a diploma should be about.

"He was excited about Sicilian cooking the other day, so we said that maybe he could actually go to Sicily and study cooking for his senior project. Suddenly he was excited about learning to speak Italian. He might not follow through, of course, but if we're good at our job then we'll just keep making those connections and maybe one of them will work. For now I'm going to cut him some slack if that's what it takes to keep him in school. I'm also going to make sure he sees doctors about why he can't sleep at night. Schools usually ignore that kind of thing, but it's incredibly important."

Schools that emphasize interests run the risk that students' learning will become focused too narrowly. "During the sixties and seventies," writes Herb Kohl (1998), "many teachers were discovering . . . the importance of beginning with students' interests and experiences in order to prepare the ground for other, more sophisticated learning. Unfortunately, this strategy was often taken to mean simply centering learning on student interests—to me, a condescending way of limiting the scope of learning. This was not at all what we had in mind. Education has to be as demanding as it is giving. There are many things of value in the adult world, and it is our obligation as teachers to balance children's needs and interests with exposure to the social, cultural, and technological achievements that are our gifts to them" (p. 13).

"I agree with what Herb is saying," Dennis said, "and I don't think the Met is falling into the trap he warns against. If a student is only interested in basketball, we don't have him shoot hoops for 4 years. But we might *start* there. Take Larissa for example. Hairdressing is not a field we typically push our students toward, but that was her interest, so she got an internship with a hairdresser. Then her advisor guided her toward a book about Madame C. J. Walker, an entrepreneur and social activist who had made a million dollars in the hair care industry. It was Larissa's first connection to Black adults who have succeeded financially. It got her excited, and she gave a great report on it. Not long after that, one of our staff members who was going to Little Rock for the anniversary of desegregation held an essay contest to select a student to join her. Larissa was still inspired from her research on Madame Walker, so she wrote an essay that won the contest. Then she had some amazing experiences in Little Rock that got her even more excited about learning. Eventually she did a series of projects on gestational diabetes and domestic violence. In her graduation speech she said,

'I went from hair care to human repair.' And it all started with hairdressing.

"We're trying to find the way for each student to learn the most, so we expand outward from their interests. That's limiting in some ways, of course, but every approach to education is limiting—it's just a matter of how you decide to limit. I hire teachers who are lifelong learners and broad, smart people, so I know that they'll constantly be exposing students to things that go beyond their immediate interests. Students are always reading the newspaper and discussing it in advisory. Advisors are always raising provocative questions, putting vocabulary words up on the board, or bringing their students to a museum. They do it in a million ways."

A second passage from Kohl's (1998) book discusses a high school class he taught in which students planned a response to an imaginary earthquake. Their job was to resettle 8,500 displaced people onto a designated parcel of land. "The class was to be a flowing stream," Kohl wrote, "always subject to the creative input of the participants. However, I didn't want to step into the water the first day of class and let everyone be swept away by their first impressions and wildest ideas. I believed the students ought to have certain tools before they embarked on the planning, and some conversations about the issues we'd be considering. Many child-centered and progressive educators would disagree with me on this issue, believing that all the skills of thinking and researching should emerge from project learning and the students' experiences. I find it easier, more systematic, and more effective to do direct teaching once in a while or to set a topic for conversation that none of the students could possibly decide on" (p. 278).

"I believe in doing whatever works," Dennis said in response to this passage, "and that includes guiding students to whatever resources they need. If they're going to use it right away, like in Herb's class, it can work pretty well. But generally I argue against making students learn something they won't need until much later, because in my experience it hasn't worked for most students. A lot of our students take college courses, and we've talked about requiring them to do a note-taking workshop just before the course starts. They're about to need the skill, so why wait until 2 weeks into the course when they start failing? If we introduce it ahead of time and it works, then clearly that's the best way to go. But if it doesn't work, I would argue that it's because the students don't feel the need yet. Maybe we should watch carefully and give it to them just when they realize how badly they need it—like on the fourth day of their college course. In a small school like ours you can do things like that.

"Another example is one of our seniors who was in legal trouble. He told me he was going to reject the court-appointed lawyer and defend himself instead. So I told him 'Don't do it—you could crucify yourself up there! Even if you don't like the lawyer, he can make better deals than you.' Half of our students come up against the law at some point, so part of me thinks we should be teaching every student how to deal with that. But they all think that *they'll* be the ones to avoid getting arrested, so will they hear it if we teach it? Then there are some things that we *do* teach everyone, like preventing AIDS and pregnancy, even though they don't think *that's* going to happen to them either. I have no problem with teaching something to all students at the same time if it's going to keep a student from burning his hand, or if we're truly teaching it successfully rather than just kidding ourselves. But so many schools are teaching content that students just aren't hearing. If students aren't interested and engaged, then most of them aren't going to be learning."

4 Learning Through Internships

One evening on the commuter train, I chatted with an entrepreneur whose son David was failing out of his suburban high school. Private tutoring wasn't helping, and the son refused to create more study time by quitting his after school job at a bait-and-tackle shop.

Then I heard the details of the job. David had built a close relationship with the owner, who was ready to retire. While David's friends splurged on used cars, David had banked $12,000 of earnings and had negotiated with the owner to buy the shop in 6 months when he turned 18. He believed that he could increase profits dramatically by increasing sales even slightly, because the store was hovering near the break-even point. With his father's help, he had drafted a marketing plan that they believed would boost sales and triple profits once he took over the shop.

And this is a student who is failing high school. If David had been at the Met, his work at the bait-and-tackle shop would have become his internship—the hub of every student's curriculum. The marketing plan would have been a starting point for studying math, computers, and English. Other studies might have focused on the physics of a fishing rod or the social and economic impact of a local oil spill. David's father was crestfallen when I told him, as we pulled into the Providence train station, that his son was probably too old to transfer to the Met.

Chasing Darth Vader[1]

MediaTech has a tidy sales counter up front and a computer-strewn workroom out back. Three programmers sit shoulder to shoulder,

---

1. Julie Gainesburg generously allowed me to adapt the following two vignettes from unpublished materials she wrote for The Big Picture Company.

each intent on a computer screen. They're behind schedule on a graphics CD-ROM that must be Fed-Exed to a major corporation in 6 hours. A customer walking into the store would never know that one of the programmers is a ninth grader.

Jamar's passion was computer graphics, so, with help from his advisor, he found MediaTech for his ninth-grade internship. (Met internships are known as LTIs, an acronym for Learning Through Internships.) Bill and Edward—MediaTech's founders and only two employees—were relieved to have another partner for their start-up company. For the first few weeks Jamar helped them figure out new software packages and design custom graphics. After that, he sat down with Edward and his Met advisor to plan a multimedia project that would strengthen the company's marketing efforts.

"Ever since I saw *Star Wars Special Edition*," Jamar's proposal began, "I've wanted to learn graphic design and create 3-D special effects myself. I've already started by designing a little 3-D guy who walks around on the computer screen.

"For my LTI project, I'm going to create a multimedia production that displays MediaTech's full capabilities to its customers. First, I will learn a lot about what each of MediaTech's application programs does and why they use it. Some of my questions are: What type of market is MediaTech trying to target with their products? How can I create a product that is better than industry standards? What *are* the industry standards? How can you design an interface that can be changed while the program is up and running? And many smaller questions that are still waiting to be found."

In addition to graphics skills, Jamar's project required math, logic, and communication. Back at the Met, his advisor supported each of these needs. "Some of the math was hard for him," she says, "especially being able to *explain* what he was doing. That's something we emphasize at the Met. Sometimes Jamar will write something that is brief and well crafted, but if you don't know enough about computers then you don't understand what it means. So I push him to break it down and walk me through."

Sitting in front of his computer one day, Jamar hit a major snag and Edward slid over to help. They spoke quietly, plumbing each other's intertwined knowledge of the project. Jamar moved to Edward's computer and began checking an Internet database.

Then Edward asked Jamar to check something in a manual. A while later Jamar identified the problem and told Edward what to change. They had spent the morning as colleagues, completely focused on thinking and problem solving.

In junior high school, Jamar lost papers, forgot assignments, and couldn't get organized. These problems began to improve at Media-Tech when he began to suffer the real world consequences of being scattered. "His projects would fail because he had jumped right in without the proper planning," Edward says. "He got really frustrated, so now he's learning to think things through before he starts."

One evening in mid-March, Jamar presented his multimedia project to the adults on his learning team. Afterward, his advisor wrote, "Jamar has learned a tremendous amount. He has become more confident, serious, and focused, but he needs to improve on using his daily planner to manage projects and appointments. He is learning the beauty of designing a meaningful education for himself. His mentors have entrusted him with real work, and he has taken that opportunity and run with it."

"It makes me feel so proud of my son," Jamar's mother added. "He's become so valuable to MediaTech. That's why he's working hard now—because he feels important and valued. After the exhibition he talked about his future goals for the first time ever, about going to college. He mentioned MIT and the Rhode Island School of Design. We had never talked about that before. I was really touched. I just looked at him and thought 'Wow!'"

Edward wasn't surprised to hear Jamar talking that way. "Jamar is learning the crucial, hands-on stuff that we can't even find in the college graduates we interview. Not to mention that he's using our cutting-edge equipment, while college kids are paying top dollar to learn on obsolete systems. A lot of RISD kids come in here to get things printed, and they're amazed when Jamar shows them what he's doing. They ask him 'What college do you go to?' It's kind of funny."

Getting Physical

The sunny main room at Atlantic Physical Therapy has massage tables, a lumbar pillow with Holstein cow spots, and a berry aroma wafting from a candle. Solana's fascination with physical therapy began after her mother had knee surgery. She called dozens of physical therapists and found an LTI by October.

Solana's mentor was Esther, the clinic manager and a natural teacher. Solana attended consultations, helped patients with exercises, did office work, served as a Spanish interpreter, and worked out on the exercise equipment. She wanted to learn more about health and science, so Esther suggested a project on fibromyalgia, a painful syndrome that afflicted many of the clinic's patients. Esther had been meaning to assemble some educational materials for these patients, but she hadn't found the time.

After some research and fine-tuning, Solana wrote, "My project is to develop a pamphlet on fibromyalgia and stress management. I will look at causes, prevalence, demographics, symptoms, and physical therapy. When people learn to manage stress well, their fibromyalgia often improves or even goes away. I need to read the articles I've gotten from Esther and the Internet, interview a doctor, make a printing budget, and learn PageMaker publishing software. Esther is depending on me getting the pamphlet out to her patients."

Solana also made forays into anatomy, physiology, and kinesiology. "We talk about those topics with patients all day," Esther explained. "Bones and muscles, ligaments and tendons. The three types of levers in physics, and how your body becomes part of the lever. Why lift with your knees instead of your back? How do people conserve energy when they're moving through space? Each day I show Solana something about the science underlying my work with patients, and then I give her pages from my textbooks to study with her advisor Emily back at school."

A key communication tool between Solana and Emily was the journal that Met students are expected to write in three times per week. It motivated Solana to jot down thoughts or questions whenever they came up, rather than waiting until Emily was available. Then Emily would respond in person or comment in the journal.

One day Solana's journal entry said, "Did I tell you that I called the community college and they have a program to train physical therapy assistants? I am ZOOPED! They're going to mail me some info. I hope I can do it. Now onto my project and its progress:

Stuff I have done!

- Wrote first draft of pamphlet
- Called copying places for estimates
- Started the outline and introduction for my project paper
- Sent the questionnaire to the doctor (I just hope he actually fills it out!)
- Did my project timeline

Stuff I still need to do...

- Finish, edit, and type the pamphlet and my project paper
- Do PageMaker graphics for the pamphlet
- Call the Centers for Disease Control for fibromyalgia statistics
- Do a demographics graph in Microsoft Excel
- Do the visuals and rehearse for my exhibition."

Many 10th graders were studying algebraic functions at that time, and they had to use charts, graphs, and formulas to show relationships among variables drawn from their LTI projects. Working with Emily and the Met's math coordinator, Solana did an experiment to find out how torque varies as patients lift heavy objects at various distances from their body. "My hypothesis was that the further your arm is away from your body the easier it will be to lift something," Solana explained. "My experiment showed how wrong I was. Now I know that the formula for torque is pounds times distance, so more distance means more torque and the object gets harder to lift."

Three days before her final exhibition, Solana got bad news. The clinic had reorganized and Esther was out of a job. "Her exhibition was supposed to be all authentic at the clinic," Esther said, "and now we couldn't do that. Solana still had lots of questions, so I gave her my home phone number and she called me like 16 times. But all the work was worth it. I wouldn't have missed it for the world."

Despite the sad turn of events, Solana's exhibition was festive and well-attended. She looked professional in a white skirt and orange blazer, standing behind a table piled with her fibromyalgia pamphlets. She discussed the disease, showed overheads, and then brought her mother up front to demonstrate the torque experiment. After some questions from the audience, the formality gave way to congratulations and sadness about the end of her special relationship with Esther.

"The Met wanted Solana to learn academic and personal skills through her work with me, but not necessarily to become a physical therapist," Esther said after the exhibition. "But then one day she announced that she wanted to become a physical therapist, and after that her motivation really changed. Now when she doesn't know something, she pushes to learn more and more."

Learning Through Real Work

The Wiesner Building at MIT has an oddly decorated exterior, a pattern of white squares with black outlines. One of the exit doors is blended so carefully into the pattern that a casual passerby notices only the wall, not the door. Once, sitting in the adjacent pavilion, I was startled to see the wall open and a person emerge. Only then did I notice the hinges.

An important role of LTIs is to open hidden doors in what appear to be walls. One time when I visited a student's LTI, she was engrossed in writing a grant application to obtain funding for her host site. She was 15 years old. The first time I applied for a grant, I was nearly twice her age. Until then, grant-writing was a daunting mystery. But Met students learn early on that with hard work they can gain access to many of the world's elusive resources.

"Things really take off when students find an LTI they love with a mentor they love," Dennis says. "That's when they get the most out of the Met. For 20 years I was the principal of schools with caring advisors and interesting projects, but it wasn't enough. When students do all their projects inside the school building, their inspiration eventually drops off. But when they work in real-world settings with a great mentor, they shoot up to the next level. They get so proud and their learning takes on such meaning for them. We've had dozens of students who were ready to drop out until they got turned on by an LTI. And students who are already thriving get turned on too.

"Two of our students who have been in trouble on the street come to mind. John had an LTI at the coroner's office, so it's a very serious place. One day his mentor was at the Met and saw him running down the hall fooling around. The mentor couldn't believe it was the same kid—and it *wasn't* the same kid. They're different when they're out in their LTI sites. Then there's Martin, who has an LTI at a middle school. He does lunch duty there, and he told me very earnestly, 'I'm a *counselor* for all those kids.' It's so perfect for a kid like him. At lunch duty all the kids want to talk to him and get his advice about their problems. And I bet he's really helping."

On average, each Met student has one LTI per year. It begins in the fall, meets during school hours on Tuesday and Thursday, and lasts for 5 or 6 months. But that's only an average. LTIs have lasted from 3 weeks to 3 years, started in April or August, and taken place on all days of the week. Some LTIs have crunch times when students spend 40 hours per week at the host site, and some students spend an entire year without having an LTI at all. (They do other types of projects, as described in the next chapter.) The Met's flexible schedule is designed to accommodate the ebb and flow of personalized projects and real work.

LTIs combine the "academic" and the "vocational"—labels that drive an illusory wedge between two deeply intertwined domains. When properly designed, hands-on learning can lead to academic learning, as the LTIs of Jamar and Solana illustrate. Moreover, LTIs are not vocational. They are designed to foster general skills, not to prepare students for specific vocations. One student did LTIs with a computer programmer, a judge, and a dance instructor.

Giving students the opportunity to follow different interests over time is essential to the Met's approach. "In that respect, we're very different from career academies," Dennis says. "Career academies are getting more popular in the United States, but the problem is that most of them attach students too strongly to a single vocational track—management or computers or something else. One student at the Met did two culinary LTIs but then got interested in politics and did two great LTIs with lobbying groups. At a career academy, it would have been very difficult for him to make that switch."

A prominent evaluation of 10 career academies supports these concerns, reporting that about one out of four students lost interest in their academy and left before graduation. An additional group of students (percentage not reported) stayed until graduation but

never took part in work-based learning activities because they opt-
ed not to, failed to meet the academy's eligibility criteria, or
couldn't be placed due to the limited number of available slots
(Kemple, Poglinco, & Snipes, 1999).

Learning through doing is as old as humanity. The artificial rift
between classroom and hands-on learning is a modern invention
whose fallout is becoming apparent. Researchers and employers
are finding that students—even those who have earned top grades
in challenging courses—often make fundamental errors when
asked to apply their classroom knowledge to real world situations
(Gardner, 1991).

Textbooks seldom pitch the curve balls of real life, so students
don't learn how to swing at them. Instead, they sit alone at their
desks and work through neatly packaged problems. The teacher
already knows the answers, and the "right" strategy just happens
to be found on the textbook pages that were covered in class that
day. In contrast, solutions to the significant problems of real life
are unknown at the outset and often require collaboration with
others. They usually involve searching for information, devising
and modifying strategies, and persevering until the problem has
been solved or abandoned.

Solana's original project was to figure out why her mentor
was seeing more cases of fibromyalgia in Rhode Island than she
had seen at a previous job in Florida. She searched the website
of the Centers for Disease Control and Prevention, contacted a
fibromyalgia specialist (who never responded), and spoke with
personnel at the Florida Census Bureau, the Arthritis Foundation,
and the American Fibromyalgia Association. Eventually she concluded that the data she needed didn't exist. But in the process
she developed research skills and learned how to change directions
after facing an insurmountable problem.

Modern cognitive scientists have demonstrated the importance of combining hands-on learning with more conventional approaches. Howard Gardner's research shows that humans have
many "intelligences"—ways of learning about and interacting with
the world. The eight he proposes are linguistic, logical-quantitative,
spatial, musical, bodily, interpersonal, intrapersonal, and naturalis-
tic (1999). Most schools emphasize just two of these intelligences—
linguistic and logical-quantitative. This narrow focus harms not

only those students whose strengths lie elsewhere, but also those whose strong linguistic and logical abilities mask important deficits in other areas.

LTIs are designed to tap all eight intelligences and take advantage of their synergy. Phil had a keen mind and was passionate about boating and carpentry, but he was unable or unwilling to learn from books on those topics. His LTI was at a yacht restoration school. His mentor began by saying, "Here's some wood. Spend some time with it. Just fool around with it and figure it out." Later Phil worked on various yacht design and repair projects. Before long, his Met advisor noticed that Phil was able to discuss and write about woodworking in ways that had previously eluded him. Paradoxically, his route to better linguistic skills had been more spatial than linguistic. Similar crossovers happen often, as with Cesar's work at a recording studio or Shawn's acrobatics with a traveling circus.

"Many times you have to let go of the academic to get to the academic," Elliot says. "We're slowly coming to understand this. Too often we're uptight and don't let students feel their way through. Most of us have gone through conventional schooling, and we're trying to change our world view to trust different ways of doing things. Lots of students just won't succeed using traditional methods, even though they're intellectually powerful with their hands or in other ways. And even with students who *can* get there the traditional way, we *still* need to do the real-world piece. Once they've actually *used* calculus, they move to a much higher level of ability and understanding."

In his book *The Hand*, neurologist Frank Wilson traces the evolution of the hand and its influence on culture and learning. Consistent with the Met's philosophy, he argues that schools make a critical error by sequestering students in classrooms where knowing is separated from doing.

"The hand speaks to the brain as surely as the brain speaks to the hand," Wilson says. "The old mind-body separation does not stand up to careful scrutiny, even when one considers the most complex forms of culturally derived behavior. High levels of achievement in purely 'physical' skills like juggling and competitive athletics depend on a mastery of both procedural and declarative knowledge, and achievement in those domains follows the same developmental course observed among highly successful mathematicians, sculptors, and research scientists. The clear message from biology to educators is this: The most effective methods for cultivating intelligence aim at uniting (not divorcing) mind and body" (1998, pp. 289, 291).

"That's why we have LTIs," Elliot says. "Knowing informs doing, but doing also informs knowing. Both parts are essential, but conventional schools mostly ignore the second part. Whether it's basketball or biology, students need to spend some time *doing* in order to really understand."

LTIs may have an additional advantage for students who enter the work force directly after high school. A survey of 3,000 American companies showed that most are "afraid to hire young people, viewing them as unreliable workers" (Schorr, 1997, p. 293). This becomes a self-fulfilling prophecy for many recent graduates whose eagerness and persistence fade after years of drifting through several low-wage, dead-end jobs. The Met believes that skittish employers will be reassured by students' LTI experiences and by endorsements from satisfied LTI mentors.

Finally, LTIs bring youth into closer contact with adults inside and outside the school. Summarizing several prominent reports on American education, Cremin (1976) notes that 20th-century high schools "managed increasingly to isolate young people from the rest of society, organizing them into rigidly defined age groups . . . that have little contact with either younger children or adults. In the language of one report, the schools have effectively 'decoupled the generations.' As a result, the reports conclude, the ordinary processes of socialization have been weakened, confused, and disjointed, and the symptoms are everywhere apparent" (p. 63). Cremin then cites a series of proposed reforms "all designed to increase opportunities for children to associate with adults in realistic social situations where they could undertake genuine responsibility for worthwhile tasks" (p. 65). That is the heart of learning through internships at the Met.

Finding and Developing an LTI

Finding an LTI starts with exploring interests, as described in the previous chapter. Students do research to identify people who are involved with the student's interests. Then they develop lists of questions and interview the people they've identified. This process helps students find LTIs while also building life skills such as persistence and presenting themselves well.

Shadow days are the next step. After a student identifies a potential LTI site, she spends a day there "shadowing" the person who would be her mentor. The Met offers these suggestions to the potential mentor:

- Provide a workplace tour and describe your organization's main objectives.
- Tell the student why you chose your work and why it's important to you.
- Demonstrate your work rather than just talking about it.
- Share what you do to keep up-to-date in your field.
- Explain how your work fits in with the overall organization.
- Show them the fun side—laughing together is a great equalizer!

Some students do several shadow days before finding an LTI that interests them. Most find an LTI by November, but for others it takes longer. "Loretta was scared to make calls," her advisor says. "With the help of a fellow student, she set up informational interviews with some stores she liked at the mall. I gave her the name of someone there who had mentored another Met student, but she had left for another job by the time Loretta called. Loretta was so upset that she walked out of school for 2 days. After that she refused to make calls for a few weeks until her friend stepped in to help. Eventually she did some interviews that went well, but right before her first shadow day the business called it off because of her grunge-style clothing. Loretta was devastated. She's a great artist though, and in the end she got an LTI with a graphic design company."

"We need to do a better job with students who are struggling to find an LTI," Dennis adds. "If it's taking a while, we should be quicker to get them doing other kinds of projects. Take a student like Tony, who dropped out of high school 2 years ago and is just returning. It's taking him too long to find an LTI, and we're losing him. We need to work together as a staff for students like him. We need to discuss their interests, shoot out lots of different ideas for

LTIs, and then help them follow up on as many leads as possible. We have lots of ways to help students learn through their interests, but we believe that LTIs are the best way. So for the few students who just won't do what it takes to get one, even with the tremendous support we give them, it's a problem. We're now requiring students to have at least one serious LTI before they can be promoted to 11th grade."

LTI development is supported by the Met's workplace coordinators. They cultivate relationships with local organizations, help advisors find LTI sites, train and support mentors, collect data and write reports about the LTI process, and develop personal and academic relationships with many Met students.

Once the student identifies a potential LTI site, the Met decides if the mentor is a good match with the student, and if the workplace would be an appropriate learning environment. Potential mentors speak with the student's advisor, watch a 15-minute video, and receive a notebook describing the LTI process in depth. They also agree to undergo a background check, and on the few occasions when it has revealed a criminal record, the school and parents have decided together about the appropriateness of the placement.

There is no ideal mentor profile. Inez and her mentor were both bubbly and loved chatting when time permitted, whereas Jamar's soft-spoken style meshed better with his mentor's quiet intensity. But dissimilar styles can be productive too—an outgoing physician helped Julia overcome her shyness, a formal banker helped Miguel tone down his smooth talk, and a no-nonsense chef occasionally succeeded in pressuring Tony to finish his schoolwork.

The first few weeks of a new LTI are for the student to begin getting to know the people and routines of the host site. Then the student, mentor, and advisor begin planning a long-term project that benefits the host site and advances the student's learning goals. These projects have three elements: (1) an end product for the host site, (2) the investigation related to that product, and (3) the student's critical reflection on the learning process. The Met calls these three elements the "nested egg," a label poached from the children's toy of the same name. As explained in the Met's curriculum materials, "the nested egg places the real work for the LTI site at its center. Investigation surrounds that work, and reflection encompasses the whole project." The nested egg label refers not only to LTI projects, but also to the other types of projects discussed in the next chapter.

One day I shadowed Maya, an 11th-grade advisor, during visits to the LTI sites of four students in her advisory. The first stop was an upscale café, where Luther was dressed in a white chef's outfit. His project was to use the scientific method to reduce the calories and saturated fat of several recipes without sacrificing taste or aesthetics. Using FDA nutrition guidelines and dietary software, he proposed recipe changes that seemed promising. Then he cooked the modified recipes, analyzed the results, and tweaked the dishes through several rounds of improvement.

Next we drove to Kaufman-Parlow Architects, where we met with Lucia and her mentor in a newly furnished conference room filled with blueprints for a new housing development. At this same LTI the previous year, Lucia developed a scale model of the Met's new campus. The project used skills that she had just acquired from two college classes on architecture and computer-aided design. This year she's helping to draft floor plans for a nearby clinic. When Lucia arrived at the Met, she was withdrawn and tongue-tied, but her passion for architecture gave her direction and self-confidence. In 11th grade she spoke about the Met at an educator's conference and later won a $5,000 scholarship in a national design competition for high school architects.

Next we drove 20 miles west, into forests and farmland. Cathy's LTI is with a retail store that sells horse-riding equipment. Her dream is to be a horse trainer, but she knows it doesn't pay well, so she chose an LTI that would expose her to the business side of riding. She hopes to spend her life around horses while still earning a good living. Walking past ornamented saddles, riding crops, and the Jackasses 2000 wall calendar, we found Cathy and her mentor Lena with the store's account ledgers spread out on the front counter. Cathy's project was to learn the store's accounting software and then write a training manual for future employees who need to use the software.

The phone rang, and Lena answered it. "Good afternoon. . . . Yes, we sent that out yesterday—you'll have it very soon. . . . Bye bye." Lena turned to Cathy and rolled her eyes in amused exasperation. "It was that saddle sale—I *told* you they'd call!" They both laughed at the inside joke, and a flicker in Cathy's private eyes betrayed her pride at being in the know.

Then a second project idea emerged. Lena needed to decide which Florida horse shows to attend, based on several aspects of each show that affect her profit. Maya suggested that Cathy could learn Microsoft Excel back at school and design a spreadsheet that would estimate the profitability of different shows. Lena quickly agreed, saying maybe it would be good for business. "Sometimes I forget that you're only 17 years old," she said to Cathy. "Maybe someday we'll have a job for you here doing the books."

Back on Route 95, we landed in a traffic jam. We took the first exit and Maya phoned ahead to say that we would be late. Isabel's LTI was with the parent liaison at a local elementary school. Her first language is Spanish, so she helps with oral and written translation for conferences, home visits, and report cards. She still struggles with basic literacy, and working as a translator has helped. During our meeting, two project ideas were hatched. First, Isabel would collect data on family involvement at the school and graph month-to-month changes in response to new outreach efforts. Second, she would interview the parent liaisons at five nearby schools and prepare a paper on effective practices that her host school might benefit from trying.

Six hours after Maya and I set out, we returned to the school. She had helped her students launch projects, but her job was far from over. Advisors also need to build relationships with the mentor and host organization in order to keep the partnership productive over time.

At one LTI meeting, the mentor arrived very upset. The Met had thrown a celebration to honor mentors but had accidentally mailed his invitation to the wrong address. Their mistake had cost him an opportunity to be honored in front of some high-level city officials—exposure that could have helped his business. Afterward the Met sent a card saying, "We are so sorry for our mistake. If it's any consolation, please see on the enclosed program that your name was listed as one of our honorees." But the program wasn't enclosed, and the mentor was irritated. For 2 years he had carved mentoring time out of his frenetic schedule, and he deserved better treatment. Waving the empty card at the advisor, he muttered something about an infected root canal and said, "So let's get started."

At that moment it was the advisor's delicate task to preserve the relationship, and fumbling it wouldn't have been difficult. But with grace, sincere apologies, and superb people skills, she steered the meeting into calmer waters. Relationships with LTI mentors aren't usually that thorny, but the advisor's success still depends on a broad repertoire of knowledge and skills. A short list includes:

- convincing busy people of the rewards of mentoring;
- understanding the mentor's personality and workplace;
- using that understanding to shape the LTI in productive directions;
- helping mentors identify projects that benefit both the students and the site;
- conducting meetings that balance congeniality with task orientation; and
- helping mentors create appropriate structures for the student's learning.

The Power of Mentoring

During my visit to Luther's LTI, it became clear that he had not planned his work well and was now feeling overwhelmed. His advisor asked him to take out his notebook and begin fleshing out a work plan and timeline.

Then his mentor jumped in: "Believe it or not, you're ahead of the game. I didn't learn how to organize my work or anything else in my life until the end of 12th grade. When my list gets too long, I start feeling overwhelmed and paralyzed, just like you're feeling now. But once you have an outline and a plan, it's like having a road map—you start knocking off one thing after another, and you start feeling better."

Luther's stress level decreased visibly, and suddenly he was talking about the importance of planning and getting organized. His Met advisor had offered similar advice many times, but coming from the mentor it took on renewed meaning.

Research has consistently shown the social and educational benefits of surrounding children with caring adults who spend quality time with them (Herrera, Sipe, & McClanahan, 2000). The relationship between student and mentor is thus a vital component of every LTI. Ideally, the mentor becomes an additional source of the respect, warmth, and support that the Met strives to provide for all of its students. Mentors are encouraged to be both teacher and parent, much like Met advisors. More than just imparting knowledge, they help students develop life skills and often become invested in the student's success in life.

"I helped Miguel become more professional," says Cecil, his mentor at Heritage Bank. "I taught him that when you work in a bank you have to dress the way bankers dress. One day he came in with his shirt undone and his tie hanging down, and I told him to walk out and try again. He wasn't happy, but he did it. Now he dresses professionally and sees that he gets more respect. We're slowly working towards having him create a system for tracking and monitoring our accounts receivable. We're not setting small goals here. We figure we'll shoot high."

At Community Networks, director Anne Smith remembers that "at first Carlita didn't understand that showing up meant more than being a warm body. It means being productive, preparing for team meetings, and finishing your work—because people are *relying* on you. At school, showing up unprepared only hurts *you*. But our work is highly team-focused, so when you're unprepared it hurts everyone. She learned those lessons quickly and made great contributions to the team."

Mentors also help students by debunking romantic images of certain career paths. Tamika's final project at the Providence Black Repertory Theater was a research paper on famous Black female vocalists. She discovered that even superstars like Billie Holliday had faced oppressive uphill struggles. The next year she did an LTI with Flora Cooper, a one-woman entertainment company. "Flora taught Tamika the self-discipline things before teaching her the fun stuff," says Tamika's advisor. "She had to make flyers, type things, and do research. Only then did Flora teach her how to exercise her diaphragm and use her voice well. She learned that even something as glamorous as the entertainment business has its tedious behind-the-scenes work that you have to be disciplined to complete."

At the equestrian store where Cathy was doing her LTI, she learned that her mentor hadn't had a day off in 2 years. "That's what it takes to get a business off the ground," her mentor said. "My love for riding horses is why I started the business in the first place, but I don't even have time to ride anymore! The horse shows are great, and that's where I make most of my money, but being on the road gets exhausting after a while. Things are finally getting a little easier—after 2 years I'm beginning to make a profit and hire some help."

These reality checks also help to clarify student values. During Julia's LTI at the zoo, she realized that her views on animal rights conflicted with her ambition to become a veterinary researcher. Her interests quickly shifted away from veterinary medicine and toward pediatrics.

I envied her early wake-up call. It wasn't until my final year of college that two incidents jolted me away from electrical engineering. First, I toured a weapons facility and was offered a job designing night sights for cruise missiles. Most job openings in electrical engineering were defense-related at that time (Berlin was still divided and the Internet boom was years off), but I had never been close enough to the technology of warfare to experience the revulsion it evoked in me. Touring the facility changed my long-held stance that "someone else will build weapons if I refuse, so my refusal is meaningless." The second jolt came during a summer co-op job, when I had to scrap several days of work because the circuit I had just designed was too slow by less than one billionth of a second. It finally became clear to me that despite the status, salaries, and stock options, these were not the problems I wanted to spend my life solving.

Such experiences come far too late for many students, even those in vocational schools. School-to-career expert Larry Rosenstock notes that only 27 percent of high school students who are trained for specific careers ever spend even a single day in their chosen field or a related one (in Washor, 1999). The Met hopes that first-hand exposure will help students develop a more realistic sense of the world's challenges and become motivated to learn.

Making LTIs Work

Before the Met's design was approved by the state, one of the toughest challenges was convincing legislators that enough adults would volunteer to become LTI mentors. Elliot likes to point out that Rhode Island has 13 adult workers for every high school student, and that more than 400 mentors have already worked with Met students. There's no mentor shortage yet, but the upper limit of their availability is still unknown.

"Being a good mentor takes way more time than we realized at first," Dennis says. "It's hard to have a kid by your side and find time for meetings with the student's advisor. Some mentors find that it's too much for them. Other mentors can't get enough of it."

And since good mentoring often determines whether an LTI sizzles or fizzles, it's important to understand why mentors voluntarily add this demanding role to their busy schedules. The most straightforward instance is when the student's work dovetails with the needs of the organization. When that happens, the student's main project advances both the organization's agenda and the student's learning.

At other LTIs, the student makes a contribution to the site but not by way of his main project. Luther contributed to Dante's Café by preparing and serving food, which also advanced his goal of attending culinary school. But his main project—experimenting with the aesthetics and nutritive value of recipes—was of no value to the restaurant. LTIs like this one benefit both student and mentor, but they are not the Met's ideal. Because of the forced fit, I call these LTIs "shoehorns," in contrast to the "dovetails" discussed in the previous paragraph. Shoehorns do feature two key aspects of LTIs—following student interests and providing real-world experiences—but they also retain some of the contrived quality that LTIs are intended to avoid. The Met believes that over time, with an expanding pool of host sites and project ideas, it will be possible to reduce the number of shoehorns and to design a dovetail for almost any LTI site.

Some mentors believe that their students add value to the host site that adults are unable to provide. "We have tunnel vision," said Jamar's mentor at MediaTech, "because our ultimate task is to make money. Jamar's imagination isn't constrained by having to pay the rent, so sometimes he'll get curious and ask a really insightful question that we never would have asked. And I'll be like 'That's brilliant—I can use that!'"

Anne Smith at Community Networks adds that "none of the adults here can think like a ninth grader, so we put Carlita on projects that need a ninth-grade perspective. If you were a fly on the wall at our meetings, you wouldn't know whether Carlita was an intern or a paid staff member, except for her obvious youthfulness. Her contributions are as valuable as anyone's, and she walks away with her fair share of the work. Then, during the days when she's at school, her teachers help her build skills to make the LTI academically relevant. Whatever it takes, they make sure she's supported.

"We did have one problem though. I wanted Carlita to help us develop a survey for the kids in our Saturday program, but our research director insisted that he could do it better and faster himself. I insisted that we would end up with a higher quality product and save time in the long run if he would just invest some time working with her up front. But he couldn't fathom it. 'Just get her to do some Spanish translation,' he said. I refused, because she was up for a bigger challenge than that. To make a long story short, she put together a fabulous survey—drafting questions, collecting data, learning how to use data analysis software, and writing a report. And when she started, she didn't know how to type or even turn on a computer. Seriously. Her perceptiveness was off the chart. Better than a lot of my staff, and there are some really bright people here. It's incredible what you can get out of a kid."

"Just knowing that I was involved with Carlita helps me put my head on my pillow at night," she continued, sounding a theme that was echoed by many mentors. The following mentor comments come from an HMO executive, a retail store owner, a banker, and the director of an art gallery:

"I'm making an important investment in the community. I've always wanted to be a mentor and was delighted to find a program where I could make it part of my work day."

"If I don't break the chain and start creating other avenues for the youth in our community, then nobody will. That's my drive."

"I grew up in the projects, but I had a good family structure and there were always mentors keeping me on the right track. Now it's my chance to give something back."

"I take it seriously because I believe that these relationships can do wonders for adolescents—and they make my life richer as well."

These sentiments may sound suspect in our materialistic times, but social interest appears to motivate most LTI mentors, whether they come from nonprofit organizations, small businesses, or large corporations. Many of these organizations also view mentoring as a way of developing a high-quality work force for the future. Many Met students have landed paid summer jobs at their LTI sites, which clearly suggest their value to the organizations.

"A final motivation for some mentors," Elliot says, "is simply that they find a kid who really likes what they like. Matthew's stained-glass work is a good example. I think his mentor's main motivation was just that he takes pleasure in passing on the craft."

Despite its merits, the LTI system has obstacles to overcome in addition to those already discussed. In some cases the student has not made a meaningful contribution to the site, either because he didn't follow through on expectations or because the student, advisor, and mentor were unable to design an appropriate week-to-week role or long-term project. Occasionally a student has alienated a mentor by neglecting important duties, or, in one case, by stealing property from the LTI site. More typically, a student's missteps are small and innocent, such as when Jamar changed some settings on his mentor's computer. "He was trying to show us that he knew what he was doing," Edward says, "but it took me hours to fix. That was early on, and he quickly learned not to do things like that."

A second difficulty occurs when projects overshoot a student's abilities or a mentor's resources. "Sadly, that happens pretty often," one advisor said. "Sometimes you develop these great projects that end up falling short of the original plan. But important learning almost always happens anyway. We're realizing that you need to plan ambitious projects and then work hard to make them succeed. The most ambitious projects—whether they succeed or not—are often the most educational and exciting for students."

Planning overly ambitious LTI projects mirrors the real world, where people overcommit and then scale back. When Met students take on too much, they begin to understand their limitations and how to make commitments they can fulfill. As for mentors who overcommit and then fail to come through, three conclusions can be drawn. First, the Met should minimize this problem by continuing to refine its procedures for selecting mentors, sites, and projects.

Second, the school should avoid burning out good mentors by sending them more students than they can handle. Third is the simple fact that educating students is not the primary mission of LTI host sites. Regardless of how skillfully the Met refines its procedures, this reality will inevitably intrude on some student projects. The Met believes that such problems are offset by the advantages of work-based learning.

Finally, the Met needs more effective strategies for placing students whose LTI searches are taking too long. "Part of this problem has been a function of the school's newness," Elliot says. "It's getting easier now that the school is 5 years old, because we have mentors and host sites that like to take students year after year. We also have students who return to the same LTI they had last year, and we're always designing better procedures for getting students out. One way to avoid the lulls would be to have pre-arranged projects and sites, but that's not the Met model. Projects need to come from the student's interests and efforts. It may not be possible to get the high points without the search period, and we see that tradeoff as educationally sound. Students learn a lot from the search process, and while they're looking for an LTI they're also taking part in the Met's many other learning activities."

5 Learning Through Everything

At the Met, the word *extracurricular* is almost an oxymoron. While most schools offer credit only for a few strictly defined subjects such as math and English, the Met offers credit for almost any activity that helps students achieve the school's learning goals. To illustrate the diversity of student work, I recount below one of the many days I spent at the school.

A Day in the Life

It's Monday after Thanksgiving break, and students start trickling into school a half hour early to eat breakfast, chat, read, and surf the web. The morning staff meeting focuses on how to work more effectively with social service agencies. After some muffins and a few hurried decisions, it's time for morning assembly.

Known as "pick-me-up," the daily assembly starts with announcements and ends with a presentation. Today Leah reports on her trip to the National Youth Advocacy Conference, a gathering of "gay, lesbian, bisexual, transgender, and questioning youth." She says that in middle school she was harassed and ostracized because of her sexual orientation. This hasn't happened at the Met, and she thanks everyone for their support. Leah's advisor, knowing the topic of today's pick-me-up, invited a diversity educator who stands up and says, "I think Leah is really brave to get up in front of you and talk about this. I'm a lesbian too, and I have two daughters in the Providence schools. Could you raise your hand if you have a gay friend or relative?" Half the students and all the advisors raise their hands. She asks several more questions that deepen the discussion, and after a few minutes pick-me-up ends and students disperse to their advisory rooms.

For the rest of the day I shadow Maya, an 11th-grade advisor, and the 13 students in her advisory. Facing each other around a conference table, most students are writing in their daily planners while two others sit idly. A student crunches cereal from two mini-boxes, alternating meticulously between Apple Jacks and Froot Loops. Maya distributes a recent article from the *Providence Journal* about a 1920s massacre of 300 Blacks in Oklahoma. Each student takes a turn reading out loud to the group. "Tulsa cherishes its mix of bible belt values, graceful architecture, and boom town boosterism," the reporter writes, "but many residents oppose the newly established Truth Commission."

"Why wouldn't they want a Truth Commission?" Maya asks. "Why do you think the massacre was covered up?"

"The local people should have gone to the newspaper and demanded that the massacre show up on the front page," says one student.

"Yeah, well maybe White people *owned* all the newspapers and didn't *want* it printed!" replies another.

"If that's true, then how come we know about Martin Luther King and Harriet Tubman? Wouldn't White newspaper owners want to hide *them* too?"

"The Tulsa massacre should go back into the history books."

"I wonder how many *other* stories we don't know about!"

"How can you believe what you read?"

Now a guest arrives, a former cocaine addict who has become a social worker. Two students leave advisory to hear her talk about staying off drugs. The remaining students discuss how Tulsa could make fair reparations to the descendants of the massacre victims. The phone rings, Maya takes the call (from a hard-to-reach LTI mentor), and the discussion loses steam. Then advisory time is over, and students disperse to work on individual and small-group projects.

Still sitting at the conference table, five girls are planning a dramatization of the books *Reviving Ophelia* and *Ophelia Speaks*. With their daily planners open again, they look for common times to write, edit, rehearse, and film their production:

"I can't get that day off!" one girl says.

"Maybe we could meet at my house on Sunday?" says another.

"Would you fix your collar? It's been bugging me all day!"

Maya joins the girls to discuss a chapter from *Reviving Ophelia* on rape and sexual abuse. Then she checks in with several students in the adjoining workroom who are holding meetings, typing project proposals, or sitting on the couch reading.

At lunch time the large central meeting room becomes a temporary cafeteria, with advisors and students sitting together at some tables. Maya sits with three other advisors, an informal meeting to strategize about helping a struggling student. The student failed his end-of-year exhibition last spring and then failed the Met's summer school too, so he wasn't promoted with the rest of his advisory. It's already late November, but the advisors still hope to help him catch up by winter break. That would allow him to be promoted and rejoin his old advisory. Most promotions at the Met take place at the end of the school year, but students can be promoted at any time of year if they fulfill the requirements of their learning plan.

After lunch, Maya begins a series of one-on-one meetings with students. The first meeting is to help Luther select a paper topic for his college writing course. Maya helps him set deadlines and block out writing times in his daily planner. She offers to help with editing and reminds him to ask other students for their comments too.

While they talk, other students walk in and out of the advisory room. One student leaves for an SAT prep workshop with the Met's math specialist, then returns a minute later and announces that he'll write in his journal instead. Poking out of his backpack is a copy of Bill Bryson's *A Walk in the Woods: Rediscovering America on the Appalachian Trail*. "I'm thinking of hiking the A.T. for 2 months as part of my Senior Project," he explains.

Next Maya meets with a student who hasn't completed her work. "I forgot," the student offers flatly.

"We talked about this yesterday," Maya says.

"The book is too heavy to carry around. I either need to read it here or at home."

"That's fine. Whichever works for you."

After a few more withering exchanges, Maya says, "I need to step back for a second and say that the vibe I'm getting from you is really negative. Is something up?"

"I'm tired. I didn't get enough sleep."

"That's OK, but if we're going to have a productive meeting,

I need you to have a cooperative attitude. Otherwise I think we should reschedule for another time."

They continue. "Can you show me what you've been doing in your Spanish class?" Maya asks.

"I've been taking part in class discussions, but I don't have any notes."

"We've discussed this before. That's not enough for me to be able to assess your work. I want you to write some journal entries about your class and give a brief presentation in Spanish to the advisory."

No response.

"I'd also like you to take notes on this discussion," Maya continues. "If I'm the one writing everything down, it defeats the purpose. You need to take charge of your own learning. In real jobs, you need to be clear about assignments before the boss walks away, and you don't always have the chance to go back and ask questions."

Maya's third meeting was private, so I walked around the school and made a list of what everyone was reading:

Books & Plays

Aeschylus, *Prometheus Bound*
Julia Alvarez, *In the Time of the Butterflies*
Roger Caras, *A Treasury of Great Horse Stories*
Charles Dickens, *A Christmas Carol*
Bill Gutman, *Sammy Sosa: A Biography*
Hesiod, *Theogony Works and Days*
Stephen King, *Hearts in Atlantis*
Richard Rodriguez, *The Hunger of Memory*
Mona Ruiz, *Two Badges: The Lives of Mona Ruiz*
Gershom Scholem, *Zohar: The Book of Splendor*
Sara Shandler, *Ophelia Speaks*
John Steinbeck, *The Pearl*
Alice Walker, *The Color Purple*
Ken Weber, *Five-Minute Mysteries*

Periodicals

Forbes Magazine
Newsweek Magazine
Providence Journal

Texts and Reference Books

College Mathematics: Calculus and Analytic Geometry
Drive Right (driver's education manual)
Marlboro College Catalogue
The Norton Reader
Nursing: The Career of a Lifetime
Smart Solutions: Decimals, Fractions, Ratios, and Percents
The Torah: An English Translation

For the last half hour of the day, Maya's students return to advisory. Jonah presents his research on the School of the Americas, citing the American military's role in training Latin American dictators. After explaining that the United States denies those claims, he presents counter-evidence from human rights groups. A debate ensues about child labor, corporate interests, questioning authority, and whether the School of the Americas should be funded with American tax dollars.

After school, Maya touches base with a student who is bored with her LTI project but hasn't been exploring alternatives. The student is also in charge of the school's new high-tech weather instruments, and she says that she wants to do weather experiments that gradually get more difficult over time. "Otherwise *that* might get boring too!" she says.

"I'm not a weather expert," Maya says, "but we'll learn this together." They agree to find meteorology books at the downtown library, design experiments, and invite a meteorologist to visit.

Then Jonah walks in, wanting to discuss his LTI at Unicom. How can he use scientific reasoning for repairing computers? The outline of a project rapidly emerges. Before each repair, he will plan a sequence of diagnostic tests based on his hypotheses about what is wrong with the computer. Then he'll update his repair protocol based on the actual results of each repair. Maya requests a quick first draft of his project plan, knowing full well that a thoughtful proposal will be in her hands by Friday.

Now it's a half hour after school. Jamar walks into the advisory room and sheepishly hands a paper to Maya. It's a script that he had started writing months ago but then abandoned. During Thanksgiving break he finally picked it up again and made some progress. Maya skims the first few pages and lets out a delighted laugh. "This could be a real play!" she says. "Have you thought about where to take it next?" They discuss next steps, and Jamar goes home looking energized.

Education Cornucopia

The Met's learning strategies are limitless. Discussing all of them in this slim volume would be impossible, so below I highlight the most common ones. The previous chapter discussed LTIs, and this chapter explores a variety of other learning activities.

Service Learning

During the Met's first year, Rhode Island asked citizens to develop exhibits for the state's new history museum. Nine Met students responded by launching a year-long inquiry into museum design and local history. They worked with students and adults throughout the state, culminating in an exhibition and reception to promote the museum.

Another group of students wanted to learn about race relations. With guidance from an advisor, they researched the topic, developed lesson plans, and taught the lessons to fourth graders at a Providence elementary school.

Projects such as these fulfill many of the Met's goals for students—becoming active citizens, learning through worthwhile tasks, and developing leadership and problem-solving skills. Service learning projects also help students to discover interests and find LTI mentors. When Leslie volunteered to help with a Halloween party for children with severe disabilities, it revealed her talent and passion for that work, led to 3 years of LTIs, and helped her gain admission to a related certification program at Rhode Island College.

The Met draws a distinction between community service and service learning. Pulling debris out of a river is community service. Adding an explicit educational component—such as studying the causes of river pollution and how to advocate for environmental policy reform—makes it service learning. The Met takes that extra step whenever possible. And when service learning projects become large enough in scope, they can become LTIs if a mentor is available.

Five More Service Learning Projects

- Designing and building a wave tank for a zoo exhibit
- Serving on the mayor's antigraffiti task force
- Forming a "Keep Providence Beautiful" club that organized service projects and created environmental service clubs at elementary schools
- Tutoring elementary school students in reading and math
- Developing a crisis intervention program for the Met

Journal Writing

March 24, 1999. I'm starting to get tired of my internship at the greenhouse. I guess everything starts to get boring to me after a while. Today we planted seeds. Hopefully things will start to grow by Mothersday. (Do you celebrate Mothersday, even though you're Jewish?) I don't think I would wanna work at a nursery in the future. Next year I wanna find an LTI in car mechanics. I guess I should start looking now so in September I'll be ready to start. This year it took too long.

You asked what age I would pick if I could stay at one age for the rest of my life. I think I would choose 21. That way I can have a driver's license so I could go to the casino and the liquor store not that I'm going to drink a lot when I get older. But I really don't think that I would want to stay one age anyway because all my family members and friends will die and I'm going to be still alive. It will be a pretty boring and sad life. What if you have cancer and become bald headed and have all these pains you'll have to stay there and suffer? Well I'm going to stop now because I don't wanna be late for work. Peace.

—Jamilah

The Met uses journals to help students express ideas, concerns, and dreams. Students write about a book they read, a sermon they heard, the judge they interviewed, or problems at home and school. They write prose, poetry, sketches, diagrams, lists, and timelines. Students are expected to write three times per week, and advisors respond promptly, so journals become another strategy for personalized learning. The goal is for students to become better writers and thinkers, and to know that they have an adult who is interested in what they have to say.

"Some students really get into journals," one advisor says. "We write back and forth, and it becomes a way of saying things that you wouldn't say in conversation or in a school context. Things that happen at home, personal fears, relationship things. And I can write back in a thoughtful way through my own experience in life. So it becomes another form of mentoring."

Another advisor says, "I've always had trouble with two things—getting students to write in their journals consistently and pulling them together at the end of the day for some reflection. So I found a compelling way to combine those two activities. I started writing a prompt on the board every morning for my students to think and write about during the day. Then at afternoon advisory we'd all write for 10 minutes about the prompt (or anything else) and then go around the room and discuss the issues it raised. A few of the prompts were 'If you were stranded on a desert island and could have any three people in the world there with you, who would you choose and why?' 'The most spiritual moment in your life was . . . ?' 'Do you believe that hitting a child is an appropriate form of discipline?' We've ended up having some very thoughtful, personal discussions, like a late-night bull session or sitting around a kitchen table. And it really helped students write more often in their journals."

Five More Journal-Related Activities

- Students exchanging journals and responding to each other's entries
- Advisors sharing their own personal journals with students
- Discussing how to create the best writing environment at home
- Learning Spanish by journaling with a Spanish-speaking advisor
- Allowing students to leave the building to write

Independent Projects

Before finding their first LTI, most ninth graders do a small, school-based project. One student had always wanted to cook lasagna, so he interviewed several chefs, studied recipes at a culinary library, decided on ingredients, went shopping, cooked lasagna for his advisory, and made a presentation about the process.

Students also do independent projects if their LTI search is going slowly or if they can't find a mentor in their field of interest. "That often happens in trendy fields like music, photography, and fashion design that interest a lot of our students," an advisor explains. "Sometimes it takes too long to find a mentor who's willing to make the time commitment, so the student gets support from the school instead."

Independent projects have many of the same challenges and rewards as LTI projects. "For Cesar's photography project," his advisor says, "he wanted to capture the unique relationships among his friends. But in the end, he had little more than random snapshots. We provided lots of support and resources, but he rarely showed the self-discipline to study the techniques he needed. He didn't develop the photos in time for his exhibition, and he was unable to speak with any expertise about the parts of the camera and their functions.

"So I gave Cesar 2 weeks to improve the project and redo his exhibition. And he really did improve his project. It turns out that the pictures hadn't come out because he hadn't loaded the film right. We shifted gears because it was too expensive to start over again, and because I had underestimated how much difficulty he'd have learning to use the light meter, adjust the aperture, and all that. Instead, Cesar went through a number of photo books, picked out several pictures that he felt were powerful, and wrote a beautiful one-page analysis of each one. He discussed the symbolism of each picture and also some technical aspects of the photography—angles, lighting, and all that. It was clear that he had developed a real interest—he wasn't just getting it done to meet a requirement."

One advisor said that the most important factor in the success of an independent project is the student's level of motivation. Many students have the strongest motivation when their project affects others besides themselves. But others have been deeply engaged by activities that were for themselves only, such as learning sign language or the Linux computer operating system.

Five More Independent Projects

- Launching a candle business with a $250 startup loan from the Met
- Assembling and editing a book of student-written poems
- Teaching oneself basic electronics
- Acting in a play written by another student
- Hosting a spaghetti dinner to raise funds for a trip to Japan

Senior Projects

Educators may never slay the senior-slump dragon, but the Met has mounted a powerful defense. To graduate, each senior must plan and carry out a year-long project that benefits the student and a larger community. Robert's project promoted youth awareness of local and global hunger issues. He organized a rally and service day, raised $2,000, and collected 2,000 cans of food and 2,000 signatures for an antihunger petition. The rally was held on the steps of city hall with streets cordoned off by police, speeches from VIPs, and banners donated by corporate sponsors. The project mentor was the director of a homeless shelter where Robert had done service learning projects.

Another student wrote, directed, and acted in an autobiographical play. For Chanda's first 2 years at the Met, he immersed himself in studying astronomy. Then everything changed when his father suddenly decided to return to Cambodia and announced that Chanda—the youngest child but the only son—would be the new man of the house. Until then, Chanda had been a good student, but now he began skipping school, using drugs, and having violent outbursts. His older brothers had been killed by the Khmer Rouge, and he was terrified that his father would die in Cambodia too.

An advantage of the Met's flexible curriculum, Dennis says, is that students can study topics that meet the needs of their life. Chanda shifted his studies from astronomy to Cambodian history and politics, trying to figure out if his father was in danger. There's little doubt that he learned more and paid more attention than if he'd been required to study the wars that usually comprise American social studies curricula.

Eventually the father returned from Cambodia, but Chanda no longer recognized his authority. That's when he decided to write a play about this series of events for his senior project. With supervision from the director of the Providence Black Repertory Theater, Chanda studied playwriting and directing, wrote a nine-scene play, directed the production with six Met students including himself as actors, and performed it at the Met for an audience of 200.

To prepare for their senior projects, students develop a proposal that discusses why they want to do the project, its historical and social context, how it will fulfill the Met's learning goals and benefit a larger community, the skills and resources needed, the project mentor, a final product, a timeline and action plan, and a reference list. The proposal is due at the end of 11th grade, which allows students to begin promptly in the fall, although many students switch to a different project later. At the end of 12th grade, students write research papers and present exhibitions to document their projects and reflect on what they've learned.

Five More Senior Projects

- Creating a math group for girls who want to pursue scientific careers
- Establishing a community garden for the Met's new campus
- Helping to plan Providence's Earth Day celebration
- Creating a citywide magazine for youth artwork and writings
- Planning a week-long backpacking trip for 15 students and staff

College Classes

"When the Met first opened, people said we were soft," Dennis says. "To prove them wrong using a benchmark they could understand, we sent a few students to college classes if they had particular interests in botany or architecture or whatever. The colleges gave our students scholarships. Then suddenly it went cuckoo and we had 50 students taking college classes. On one hand, it's great for our credibility—admissions officers may not fully understand the

Met, but they understand that our student got Bs in two college classes. I also like the officialness and the reality check that college courses provide for our students about what their education will look like once they leave the Met.

"But on the other hand, I don't really understand it yet. Should every student have to take a college class? Does it have to connect to their interests? We disagree with most college pedagogy, so how much should we send our students there? And if we want students to see what college classes will be like, should we offer some of that type of learning here at the Met? We haven't figured it all out yet."

Met students have taken courses at most of the colleges in and around Providence. The Met usually requires these students to have completed ninth grade and to be meeting other requirements such as writing in their journals, doing LTIs, and making good progress toward their learning goals.

A 1998 national survey yielded three findings relevant to college classes at the Met. First, high school graduates who start college right after high school are more likely to earn a degree than students who delay college entry. Second, high school graduates are more likely to delay college entry if their parents didn't attend college. Third, the study's participants were 25 to 29 years old, and only 33% of Whites, 16% of Blacks, and 11% of Latinos had earned bachelor's degrees.[1] These findings suggest that the 70% of Met students whose parents did not attend college face daunting odds in their quest for a degree. The Met hopes that exposing students to college will demystify the experience and encourage them to enroll immediately after graduation.

Public Speaking

The first time I heard Cesar speak publicly was at a planning meeting for a new Providence charter school. The animated, personable teenager I knew was still there, but his usual street slang

---

1. National Center for Education Statistics (1999). Data on transition from high school to college is from Table 53. Data on "first generation" students is from Table 56. Graduation rates are based on multiplying the high school completion rates from Supplemental Table 59-1 by the bachelor's degree completion rates from Supplemental Table 59-3.

and cocky informality were barely detectable. His graceful transition between worlds was impressive. One reason the Met encourages students to speak publicly is to provide authentic motivation for making that transition.

When Met staff are asked to speak publicly, they invite students to share the podium. One student spoke well to a group of graduate students but also jokingly criticized the haircut of his advisor, who was speaking next. When discussing the incident later with his advisor, the student realized that he had made other inappropriate comments in the past when feeling very nervous, and he was interested in learning better ways to manage anxiety. The Met arranges these situations so that students can learn important skills when the stakes are low and the opportunities for learning are high.

Public speaking is a way of life at the Met. All students do hour-long exhibitions of their work each quarter, and they speak publicly during pick-me-ups, town meetings, and advisory discussions. They are also encouraged to make presentations to groups outside the school. It's a natural fit, because student projects often include speaking opportunities, and because the school receives many requests to speak publicly about its approach to education.

Five More Public-speaking Experiences

- Addressing the state legislature during its reauthorization of Met funding
- Making presentations at education conferences
- Teaching managers of a pharmacy chain how to display cosmetics
- Introducing General Colin Powell at a mentoring conference
- Speaking with a class of teacher trainees at Providence College

Pick-Me-Up

One advisor calls the Met's morning assembly a "preunion," because it deepens and reaffirms the school's sense of community. Pick-me-up begins with announcements and then moves on to a presentation by students, staff, parents, or invited guests. The presentations are meant to stimulate interests, showcase skills, broaden knowledge, and energize the minds of students and staff for the day ahead.

Pick-me-ups can be as simple as a student reading a poem, playing the guitar, or showing a video of a trip to Arkansas. In general they're supposed to be uplifting, but they have also included discussions of enduring social problems and visits from a 90-year old Holocaust survivor. Advisors often continue pick-me-up discussions during morning advisory, which begins right after pick-me-up ends.

Some pick-me-ups also focus on specific Met learning goals (which are discussed in detail in the next chapter). When Elliot invited me to do a pick-me-up on juggling, for example, I linked my performance to three learning goals. For the quantitative and empirical learning goals, we discussed why juggling five balls is so much harder than juggling three. We showed that throwing a ball 100% higher yields only 41% more air time, and we discussed some of the math and physics underlying that phenomenon. For the communication learning goal, we discussed writing poetry about one's passions. As an example, I offered this haiku about my son:

> Juggling for Jesse.
> He learned to crawl last Friday
> But sits still for this.

Part of the point was that not every poem needs to be a tour de force. Among other things, writing poetry can preserve a fleeting experience. (In fact, I can hear Jesse bumping around downstairs right now, and the haiku is evoking fond memories.)

Five More Pick-Me-Ups

- A local string quartet performing Mozart
- Students showcasing the improvisation skills they had learned with a theater group
- A Met parent discussing prison life and her job as a corrections officer

- An evangelical minister offering a sermon on nonviolence
- During Latino, Black, and women's history months, every pick-me-up centering on people and topics related to the month's focus

Summer Learning

Summer vacation holds great learning potential, but few schools focus on helping students achieve it. At the Met, finding worthwhile summer pursuits is an official part of each student's fourth-quarter learning plan. The school helps students identify and apply for summer jobs, internships, and travel opportunities.

During 11th grade, Cesar tutored students at a Providence elementary school. He began talking about becoming a teacher, and he invoked Dennis's pledge to hire any Met graduate who earns a teacher certification. To help Cesar pursue this interest, his advisor helped him get hired as a summer camp counselor for special-needs children in Pennsylvania.

"Camp Taskiagi was an experience I'll never forget," Cesar says. "I still complain about the long hours on the waterfront, but I loved it. Especially the preschool swim first thing in the morning. The water was freezing, but the little kids were just jumping in psshhhh and having a blast. They would start splashing me, and I'm like 'Oh my God! So cold! So cold!' Then I get in the water psshhhh and just start dunking them, and that was my favorite time of the day. Little kids love being thrown around, and I loved every second of doing it. I loved this tiny boy Charlie whose mom was a crack addict. After he went back home I was like 'My Charlie's not here, my Charlie's not here. If he ain't here, I ain't swimming with nobody.' I still miss him so much. It drives me crazy.

"It was hard. All these 12-year-olds already into drugs and gangs and shootings. I told them, 'A lot of my friends are in jail for drugs and all that, and I used to mess around when I was younger too. But it ain't worth it, man. It ain't worth it.' That's what Camp Taskiagi was all about. It was a hospital—I mean not really, I'm just using a metaphor. The kids were the patients, and we were the doctors. The medicine they needed was love, and that's what we gave them. We were showing them that there's other things to do out there, that you don't have to be a gangster."

Five More Summer Learning Experiences

- Working with the Providence summer job corps
- Traveling to Venezuela to learn Spanish
- Attending the Met's 4-week summer school
- Continuing LTIs that began during the school year
- Attending a summer debate school

Test Preparation

Standardized testing clashes with the Met's principles, but it is unavoidable. Most colleges require applicants to submit scores on the SAT or ACT, and all Rhode Island public school students must complete state tests on several topics. Unlike in many states, passing the tests is not required for graduation.

The Met's concerns are detailed in Chapter 7, but, in brief, the school believes that most standardized tests not only disrupt student learning but also neglect many important skills and personal qualities of a well-educated person. Overemphasizing the tests would therefore be an obstacle to achieving the Met's main learning goals. But test scores influence college admissions and public opinion, which in turn affect the Met's recruitment efforts and the state's annual renewal of the school's funding.

The Met does help students to prepare for the exams, but to a lesser extent than many schools. Advisors focus on the exams their advisees will take that year (e.g., math in 10th grade, writing in 11th grade). First, they help students understand the main types of questions and the state's scoring rubrics. Students need to know, for example, that they can receive partial credit for partial solutions. Second, advisors cover frequently tested knowledge and skills that students are unlikely to have encountered from other Met activities. One advisor estimated that students average 2 hours per week explicitly focused on exam preparation. Student outcomes on these exams are discussed in Chapter 9.

Everything Else

The Met's learning activities are numerous and ever-changing. It's impossible to discuss all of them under a few broad headings in a single chapter, but in this section I briefly mention a few more.

Outdoor experiences are part of every Met student's learning. Each advisory goes canoeing, hiking, rock climbing, bicycling, or backpacking at least once each year. The Met has also worked with Brown University to form the Outdoor Leadership and Experiential Education Program, in which Brown students go on several trips per year with Met students who have strong interests in outdoor activities. The Brown students also serve as personal and academic mentors. The Met believes that outdoor experiences strengthen the school community and build skills such as communication, cooperation, planning, self-confidence, persistence, responsibility, and physical fitness.

Student workshops arise in response to student interests, school goals, or external mandates. Some are mandatory, such as math and reading circles, but most are optional. Workshops have included photography, lab skills, persuasive writing, smoker's support, Spanish, summer planning, and many others. Some exist only briefly, such as airbrushing or CPR. Others last from year to year, such as the debate team or the state-mandated health workshop. Workshop structures vary depending on the needs and interests of participants, and they can be led by students, staff, parents, or community members.

Student committees develop responses to critical issues facing the school and give students a voice in school decisions. The Met believes that this is essential if students are to feel that the school is their community and their responsibility. Committees are also intended to help students learn skills such as setting agendas, running meetings, building consensus, and making decisions. Committees vary from year to year and have included social activities, conflict resolution, yearbook, school issues, and many others. One of the most active is the governance committee, which develops the agenda for weekly schoolwide town meetings.

Teaching One Student at a Time

With its limitless learning activities, the Met has been criticized as impractical and inefficient. "Not true," Dennis says. "Actually the Met has a more natural and logical structure than most schools. The mainstream system is deeply contrived, but that's hard to see because they've had decades to streamline and popularize their awkward procedures. Over time, I think our type of school will be easier to operate. Even more important is that conventional schools just don't work for lots of students. If you're not effective, it's irrelevant how efficient you are."

The Met's teaching methods echo a prominent study sponsored by the National Association of Secondary School Principals: "Discussions and lectures are frequently unproductive and boring to students and teachers alike. . . . A discussion is the hardest kind of class to teach well and can also be an easy way to avoid learning. Most lectures we observed lacked drama or even excitement, repeated material that was easily available elsewhere, or were discursive and ill-informed. . . . It may be more valuable for a student to infrequently encounter one intense discussion or lecture than to endure daily doses of a diet where it is well understood that everyone is just going through the motions. Less may be more.

"Reducing the number of conventional classes would allow school time to be used for more productive ends. Teachers could provide the kind of personal attention to students *at school* which parents or peers routinely provide for those students who take homework *home* and take it seriously. If courses met less frequently as conventional classes, teachers would also have more time for individual or small group tutorials, coaching sessions, or chances to connect directly with families. Everyone's day-to-day activities could be more varied and less routinized. Teacher schedules could resemble more closely the schedules of counselors and special needs instructors" (Powell, Farrar, & Cohen, 1985, p. 319).

The Met's approach exemplifies these ideas. Lectures are rare, and discussions in advisory (with at most 14 students) happen only a few hours per week. Most of the day is devoted to individual and small-group activities, and some aspects of advisors' schedules do resemble the schedules of special-needs instructors at other schools.

The Met also selects curricular materials one student at a time. Advisors offer different textbooks to different students at different times, depending on their interests and learning needs. And students use many other sources in addition to textbooks, because most textbooks emphasize breadth while the Met emphasizes depth.

"Textbooks can give a false sense of progress," Dennis says. "You know you started on page 50 and ended on page 100, but maybe you skimmed without learning anything. The Met's approach makes it difficult to measure progress in terms of things like textbook pages, and that makes some parents uncomfortable. They want their child moving to higher-numbered pages, but we need to question what's really being learned. Textbooks also tend to focus on easily testable facts rather than broader themes and ideas. And if the goal was to get students *excited* about studying a topic, how many people would recommend a textbook?"

Recently I attended a 10th-grade English class in a suburban high school on the first day of their poetry unit. Before offering a single poem, the textbook dragged students through an eight-page treatise on rhyme schemes, onomatopoeia, subjects and predicates, and even how to use the dictionary. Finally came a poem. If the snoozing 10th graders were still hungry for poetry, this kiddie meal and its pre-digested interpretation probably left their stomachs grumbling:

"Don't you hate when a thunderstorm ruins your picnic? This poem unmasks the weather demons who make it happen:

The Sunny Guy
Always predicts clear skies
But he never speaks true
When the skies won't be blue.

The Thunder Clap
Is a grumpy chap
His rainy invasions
Soak festive occasions."

Could this really be the way to create lifelong learners who will be excited about great writing? The Met prefers to start with writings that capture students' interests and resonate with their experiences. Consider these first stanzas of *New Light on Your Halo* by Ellis Paul:

Welcome to the city
Where we're rich on pride and pity
Where a school boy
Just a fool boy
Gets shot down in daylight.

A state of shock
A face down on the sidewalk
Who's seeing God
And gets the nod
To heaven like a hawk.

Who keeps the score
When the city goes to war
By guns by death by money?
A man in a black coat
Standing in the gun smoke
Sips on white milk and honey, honey.

Once students are engaged by such evocative writing, perhaps *then* is the time for a discussion of literary devices. Then again, how important is it to know that *New Light on Your Halo* has an AABBCDDEEDFFGHHG rhyme scheme? And even if this knowledge somehow helps us as adults, was there something more beneficial we could have studied instead? Many educators argue that we focus on onomatopoeia because it's easy to test and grade via multiple-choice exams, unlike the more subtle and complex aspects of good poetry. The Met wants students to experience the aesthetic and emotional pleasures of reading and to reflect deeply on the social and intellectual issues raised by what they read.

One consequence of the Met's interest-based curriculum is that students may graduate with little exposure to poetry or drama or some other genre. All students take part in reading groups, but they decide for themselves which groups to join. Inevitably they will miss out on some genre or topic or time period studied by one of the groups that they *didn't* choose. But gaps are unavoidable, regardless of the approach, and the Met has chosen to emphasize depth more than breadth.

Most schools choose the opposite compromise. The conventional curriculum has been called "mile wide, inch deep" because it rapidly covers a vast number of topics without regard for students' ability to remember or apply the knowledge later. Ted Sizer calls this "grotesque coverage—Cleopatra to Clinton by April 1, three Shakespeare plays in six weeks, evolution as one of thirty chapters in an eight-pound biology textbook—a recipe for teacher frustration, academic trivialization, and student detachment" (1999, p. 10).

"Serious use of the mind takes time," Sizer says. "If you have really high intellectual standards for kids, the overloaded curriculum has to give way. To write well requires painstaking revision, and to read deeply requires the time to go over text closely again and again. Practicing any art or any science means circling around a subject, trying this and trying that, asking questions that simply cannot be answered in a trivial way" (in Cushman, 1994, p. 1).

Met advisors recommend books that target specific interests and learning needs of individual students. "I knew I could draw Cesar into reading *The Rape of Nanking*," Hal says. "It was the vivid descriptions of violence that hooked him, but what he learned was far deeper than that. He was very absorbed with the violence in his own neighborhood, and I wanted him to understand similar problems at others times and places in history. I also knew it would pique his intellectual curiosity, which is one of his great assets."

Miguel's LTI mentor recommended *The Red Badge of Courage*, which helped the ninth grader become a more thoughtful and engaged reader. "It took me a while to read it," Miguel says, "because the last time I read a book was 4 years ago. After a few chapters, I got so used to reading that the words started flowing like I was saying it out loud. At the end of the book, I got so depressed and mad. I couldn't believe that Henry died. After all that, he died. I even read the last few chapters a second time to make sure I didn't miss something, like maybe he didn't really die. It took me so long to realize that the book actually related to me. Just like kids here in Providence, Henry went through so much to be a man just to end up dying so quick at an early age. When the book was over, I didn't want it to end. I've been looking at other books like mysteries and things to read over the summer."

Targeting books can also be effective with students who are already voracious, sophisticated readers. Julia's advisor recommended *Deadly Feasts*, a book about mad cow disease, because it combined Julia's interests in science and social issues. She devoured the book and was then motivated to write a research paper on the cruel and toxic methods used by agribusiness corporations.

Writing instruction also happens one student at a time. Tamika's advisor remembers that "when she first came to the Met, she spoke in slang *all* the time. I helped her realize that she knew African-American English, but that she also had to master a second language—standard English. That's something I didn't figure out until I got to college. I had her read *Their Eyes Were Watching God* by Zora Neale Hurston. She barely understood a word, because she didn't know Southern Black English. It helped her begin seeing the distinctions between different dialects. Then she did a glossary of slang terms and redefined them in standard English. So she'd write sentences like 'That's a bangin' hat you're wearing' and I'd challenge her to rewrite it as 'That's an attractive hat you're wearing' or something like that. It made her aware that there are other words to use, and at the same time she was having fun and building self-confidence."

Met students write papers, project proposals, self-evaluations, journals, 75-page autobiographies, and more. Instruction differs from student to student, but there are common features. "It's about finding subject matter they're excited about and helping them express it," one advisor said. "Journals are pretty much sacred ground, so I don't make any corrections. But for other types of writing students do lots of drafts, and that's where I comment on grammar, punctuation, clarity, and all that. One student's college essay sounded like a thesaurus, so I helped him cut back on five-syllable words and find his own voice. Another student had great ideas but a jumbled way of expressing them, so we worked on that. I also pair up students who have complementary strengths and weaknesses. One has great flow but terrible mechanics, and the other has great mechanics but no passion, so they help each other out and have a great opportunity to reflect on the writing process."

For topics in math and science, advisors often collaborate with LTI mentors. Julia's mentor was concerned that Julia hadn't studied chemistry: "It was a dilemma, because she lacked essential knowledge for working in a lab, and I didn't know if I'd have the time to teach her." The mentor laid out what Julia needed to know, and then Julia learned it back at school with her advisor's guidance. Soon she was mixing solutions, doing tissue cultures, and designing a project to infect liver cells with retroviruses and examine the impact on antigen expression. Rather than following the learning sequence of a conventional textbook, Julia studied the specific topics and techniques that she needed for her project.

Another dimension that distinguishes the Met from most schools is what Alfie Kohn (1998b) would call a sense of purposeful clutter versus a sense of enforced orderliness. One advisor compared the Met to a busy newsroom. Conventional wisdom frowns on such vitality, but bustling classrooms can promote learning just as surely as quiet ones can mask its absence. Indeed, readers may recall once or twice having looked attentively at a teacher while their mind was a million miles away. Rather than a rigid classroom environment, it is the Met's other structures—advisories, learning goals, exhibitions, and so on—that create order and promote learning. And the Met's rate of discipline problems is far below average (see Chapter 9), which challenges the common belief that tightly structured classrooms are inherently safer.

One advisor recounted a nightmare of wandering around the school searching for his students. He couldn't find them anywhere, and he awoke in a panic. "That wasn't a dream," another advisor joked, "it was a prophecy!" It *is* challenging for advisors to create an effective balance between structure and flexibility, and to monitor 14 students who are working on projects across the school and the city. But the Met believes that its approach yields higher quality learning, so the staff accept the added complexity.

Seemingly at odds with the Met's perspective, many readers will remember the highly structured classrooms of their childhood and the successful learning they accomplished there. The Met believes that some students would learn well in almost any environment, and that some might learn best from lectures and textbooks. But they would also argue that the lessons learned in the straight rows of our youth may not have been the most important ones, that the glittering As may not have been gold.

Then there is the ample group of students who can't or won't learn using conventional methods. For them, the Met's approach often bears fruit instead of dropouts. "One student refuses to read," Elliot says, "and it's driving his advisor crazy. He knows how, but he's refusing. In the meantime, he's demonstrating his intellectual power through his hands. He's working hard with a motorcycle design team, and his old LTI mentor wants him to come back to do blacksmithing two afternoons per week.

"So I tell his advisor to keep trying, but he's going through some adolescent stuff and unless we find just the right strategy he's probably just not going to read much right now. In the meantime let's encourage him around his interests, and let's not lose him! And of course we'll keep trying to make the links between reading and his interests. Maybe he'll learn science by studying motorcycles, but maybe he never will. We'll keep trying to find connections, but it can't always be done. If we tell him that he has to read Shakespeare to become a motorcycle racer, what kind of games are we playing? He's going to say that's bullshit, and he'd be right. Someday he might regret the decisions he's making now, but we can't force him. If we try to force him, he'll drop out—and I want him in school."

6 What Should Students Learn?

"One day a student performed this incredible monologue from *Hamlet*," Dennis says. "Other students were asking 'What's *Hamlet*, man?' And in some ways that embarrasses me. On the other hand, the monologue was done in a cool way, so now maybe a bunch of students will be interested in learning more about *Hamlet*. But the passage could have been from *Macbeth* or *Heart of Darkness*, and then the students still wouldn't have heard of *Hamlet*. You can't learn everything.

"Now don't get me wrong—I would love everyone to know all these things. At my last school, I almost had teachers spend 5 minutes a day teaching things from E. D. Hirsch's 'cultural literacy' list. Then the students would know something about Don Quixote and Florence Nightingale and Hiroshima and everything else. These things *are* important in our culture, but you can't teach all things to all kids.

"Some people think we're all supposed to be smart in the same way, but when you look around a room filled with intelligent and well-respected people, you realize that they know very different things from each other. I'm just not sure that there's any one set of facts that everyone needs to know. The point for me isn't Shakespeare or photosynthesis. I'm more interested in getting students to love learning, to track down and understand information, and to know a few things deeply. Everything connects, so if you learn one thing deeply you also learn lots of other things along the way.

"But facts and skills are different. There may not be a single set of *facts* everyone needs to know, but there are definitely *skills* that everyone needs—the ability to read, write, speak, listen, compute, interpret, analyze, evaluate, and so on. Those are the tools for *using* knowledge and gaining new knowledge. Being able to speak about

81

any single topic is much less important than learning *how* to speak passionately and properly—whatever properly means in a particular context. Same with grammar. We often correct students' grammar, and we welcome LTI mentors to do the same. We make it clear to students that there will be times when incorrect grammar will make them sound dumb to someone they're trying to impress. We're trying to help them gain opportunities and knowledge.

"We also pay a lot of attention to students who might not be going to college. We encourage all our students to go, but we also know that less than a third of American high school graduates earn a bachelor's degree by age 30. For many students, high school is the last chance to learn how to learn, so that they can take charge of their own learning for the rest of their lives. Our curriculum has to be useful for life, not just for getting into college.

"But we do require all of our students to *apply* to college. Maybe they won't go right away or ever, but having gone through the process will be helpful if they change their minds later. Another reason comes from one of our students who said he didn't want to go to college. We required him to apply, and he was accepted. That's when he admitted that he'd wanted to go all along but had decided not to apply because he was sure he'd be rejected."

The Met's Learning Goals

To help students choose among their many learning options, the Met has established five learning domains in which students must improve over time: communication, social reasoning, empirical reasoning, quantitative reasoning, and personal qualities. It may sound like quibbling to talk about "communication" instead of English, or "quantitative reasoning" instead of mathematics, but these distinctions strongly influence what Met students learn and how they learn it.

"It's no mistake that three of the learning goals have the word *reasoning* in them," Elliot says. "One of our highest priorities is for students to learn to reason effectively by grappling with the real world. That's when they're using their minds well."

The Met has not developed detailed definitions of the learning goals. Instead, the school relies on local consensus based on the broad guidelines listed below. Staff and parents agree that more clarity would make it easier to plan and assess student work, but the school has not yet provided that clarity. In part, this is because the task is difficult and the Met needs to work harder at it. But it's also because the Met focuses more on striking oil than on capping wells. "If we boil the learning goals down to some very explicit set of bullet points," Dennis says, "we're forcing clarity onto an inherently messy process. Then we'll lose the real-worldness and the wild variety where the best learning so often comes from."

Communication: How Do I Take In and Express Information?

When Andy was a ninth grader, he and his advisor began developing a series of projects related to the Vietnam War, a war that his father fought in but refused to discuss. Andy selected the Rhode Island National Guard for his ninth-grade LTI and interviewed Vietnam veterans about their experiences. In later years he researched Agent Orange, read widely about Vietnam, and attended a workshop for high school teachers on how to teach about the war. To Andy's surprise, his father finally began talking about his horrific year of search-and-destroy missions, shrapnel wounds, and tragic deaths all around him.

For his senior project, Andy planned a 3-week trip to Vietnam. He raised money from a summer job, a spaghetti supper, and donations from businesses and veterans groups. And he raised enough money to bring his father along. "When I left Vietnam," his father said, "I hoped never to go back. But Andy kept getting more and more interested, and I was proud of him. Thirty-two years later, I'm returning to Vietnam with my son." They toured battle sites and museums, interviewed civilians and former soldiers, and retraced the father's steps from decades earlier.

Andy's work required skills from the traditional English curriculum, such as grammar and literary analysis, and also nontraditional skills that the Met believes will be useful throughout Andy's life. Interviewing veterans and Vietnamese nationals taught him to communicate with diverse groups of people, formulate thoughtful questions, and listen attentively to the answers. The products of his work included not only conventional essays but also narratives, proposals, research papers, fund-raising letters, a slide show, and a website. Rather than a one-shot "oral report" heard only by his classmates, he made a series of presentations to classmates, parents, veterans, journalists, schools, and teacher trainees. And instead of relying solely on textbooks and online resources, he learned the value of gaining firsthand knowledge.

Met students also develop communication skills through discussions in their advisories. These discussions take many forms—debates, Socratic seminars, free-for-alls, and others—and become less structured as students develop better skills. One advisor described a "fishbowl" activity in which a circle of students discussed an issue while other students sat outside the circle and observed. Then the two groups switched. Afterward they discussed the content and process of the conversation. Did people support their points with evidence? How could we analyze these ideas differently? Was everyone respectful? Did some people dominate? Were there many interruptions? How we can make the process inviting for everyone?

The formal components of the communication learning goal are as follows:

- Listening
    Listen carefully to people with diverse perspectives
    Understand their meaning and respond appropriately
    Conduct effective interviews
    Be able to follow spoken instructions
    Perform active listening
- Speaking
    Converse productively with a variety of people
    Deliver effective oral presentations to various audiences
    Orally express and defend a point of view
    Give spoken instructions
    Use vocabulary and grammar appropriate to the topic
- Writing
    Write text for a variety of audiences
    Write in various formats (e.g., persuasive, scientific, creative)
    Use proper grammar, spelling, and punctuation
    Express ideas clearly and accurately
    Take notes on readings and during events

Incorporate feedback into revisions of your writing
Use writing for self-reflection
- Reading
Comprehend various types of writing
Summarize and excerpt text
Follow written instructions
Comprehend information presented visually (e.g.,
diagrams, charts)
- Foreign Language
Study a second language and the culture(s) it represents
- Computers and Multimedia
Operate a personal computer
Use word processing, spreadsheet, and database software
Use telephone, fax, e-mail, and Internet appropriately
- Creative Expression
Express oneself through fine art, music, dance, or drama
Express information visually for clearer presentations

Social Reasoning: What Do Different People Say About It?

The Met rejects the traditional division of knowledge into English, social studies, mathematics, and science. Real-life phenomena seldom fall into those tidy categories, and neither do the Met's learning goals. This section emphasizes social reasoning, for example, but much of the student work discussed here overlaps with the communication learning goal.

Many aspects of Andy's Vietnam work contributed to his social reasoning abilities. In preparing for his trip overseas, he read materials from mainstream texts and from revisionist sources such as Howard Zinn's *A People's History of the United States*. While in Vietnam he visited war museums and interviewed a North Vietnamese soldier who had fought in the conflict. Upon returning, he created a website that interpreted his experiences in Vietnam and offered critical analyses of official American publications about the war. He also began a petition to convince politicians of the value of sending veterans back to Vietnam.

"Today we visited the Presidential Palace," began one of his journal entries. "It was the home of the South Vietnamese president. In the basement there were war rooms with maps pinpointing all the major battles and enemy locations. Those maps gave me a knot in my stomach. I felt bad for the President who had to look at those maps every day and think of the soldiers who were dying. I can't imagine how he must have felt. He had to decide whether it was more important to stop the fighting—which was in his power—or to fight communism. Which *was* more important? I don't think there is a clear answer for that question. I would have hated to be in his position."

"We want students to be aware of and use multiple perspectives," says Andy's advisor. "Any time they try to understand an important issue, they should use more than one lens, not just a textbook or a newspaper article. Andy has internalized those lessons through his Vietnam experiences. Now he asks deeper questions and doesn't accept things at face value."

Leslie, a 10th grader, did an LTI at a residential program for children with profound cognitive and physical disabilities. "She was having a hard year," her advisor says, "and becoming an advocate and caregiver felt great. It pained her to see counselors talking about residents right in front of them, as if they weren't in the room. At first she didn't say much, because she was new, but now she meets with the director to advocate for changes. She always assumes that the residents understand what she's saying, even though they have no clear way to show it. She's developing a real sense of empathy and has struggled to understand each kid's unique way of communicating. Her work has involved many aspects of social reasoning—cooperation, conflict resolution, citizenship, paying attention to subtle details, and understanding diverse perspectives."

The Met's social reasoning agenda is only faintly reminiscent of the traditional social studies curriculum. My own American history course in high school hurtled from Columbus to the Cold War in 9 months. We never quite reached Vietnam (Andy would have been disappointed), but then again our tour of duty would have been very brief—a few textbook pages, a lecture or two with little room for substantive input from students, a perfunctory in-class essay, and a handful of multiple-choice questions designed to ensnare rather than edify. This approach gave us time for rapid visits to the Louisiana Purchase, the Hamilton-Douglas Debates, and countless other destinations. But I remember little or nothing about these events, even though I earned good grades.

More recently, while taking a course on teaching methods, I watched a student teacher conduct a riveting lesson on Pearl Harbor. Despite my dimness in matters historical, I was gripped by his portrayal of America's bumbling unpreparedness and Japan's fatal blunder of leaving America's resupply infrastructure intact. Most fascinating was his intimation that England knew of the impending attack but said nothing, hoping it would draw America into the war. By framing it as a fierce controversy among modern scholars, he transformed history from a dusty textbook page into a lively debate among competing interpretations. That mindframe is essential for sophistication in most disciplines.

Afterward, I applauded the student teacher's artistry. The instructor of our course agreed, but he also noted that in his own social studies classroom he gets into such interpretive issues only "if time permits," and then only for a half hour at the end of each unit. "Coverage" is still king.

The Met's philosophy is different on this issue. The school believes that knowing the names of every president is less important than realizing that they were all White males, most of them wealthy, and what that says about how the world works. They also believe that it's more valuable to study one president in depth—or one civil rights leader, social issue, or historical trend—than to study of all of them cursorily.

The formal components of the social reasoning learning goal are as follows:

- History/Past Experience
  Identify relevant historical and personal information
  Interpret this information as it relates to a problem
     or situation
- Understanding Diverse Perspectives
  Empathize with people different from oneself
  Analyze problems from various historical, cultural, and
     personal perspectives
- Citizenship
  Participate in city, school, and advisory communities

> Perform service for these communities
> Reflect on the consequences of one's work
> Avoid behavior that harms or weakens these communities

- Cooperation
  > Work with others effectively to accomplish group goals
  > Use your strengths to help others accomplish their goals
- Conflict Resolution
  > Use conflict resolution and mediation skills to help resolve real personal, interpersonal, and group problems

Quantitative Reasoning: How Do I Represent It? What's the Pattern?

Jamar's graphics work at MediaTech required him to reason with abstract quantities and break complex problems into steps. He was using advanced math concepts, such as rotating two-dimensional images to make three-dimensional solids, but he wasn't learning the conventional math terms that describe these concepts. Instead, his software manuals substituted terms such as "lathing" for "rotation." This mismatch would have hobbled Jamar on college entry exams. To bridge the gap, Jamar and his advisor took standard concepts from math textbooks and related them to concepts he already knew.

When Carlita planned a conference for Community Networks, she created a computer spreadsheet to calculate anticipated costs and thereby set registration fees. The spreadsheet allowed her to compute multiple scenarios based on unknown variables such as food prices and the number of attendees. She devised algebraic formulas and programmed them into the spreadsheet, and she also had to reckon whether the output matched her general idea of how much the conference *ought* to cost per person. Modern educators call this "number sense"—the ability to judge whether a solution is reasonable—a skill that is essential to real-world math problems but rarely discussed in most classrooms.

The formal components of the quantitative reasoning learning goal are too extensive to list here, but the main topics are arithmetic, algebra, geometry, tables, graphs, and three additional topics that are less common in high school curricula: statistics, estimation, and number sense. Some students also study pre-calculus and calculus.

The focus is less on memorization and more on understanding mathematical thinking and applying it to real-world problems.

The Met's approach reflects a growing research base that reveals a mismatch between the traditional math curriculum and the quantitative demands of modern personal and professional life. Lynn Steen (1997) shows that the advanced math courses in traditional high schools—usually trigonometry, advanced algebra, and calculus—are relevant mostly to the 5% of the population who will enter highly specialized careers such as engineering. The vast majority of high-level jobs (not just unskilled labor) require only eighth-grade math skills—arithmetic and perhaps basic algebra and geometry.

More important than advanced math skills, Steen (1997) argues, are the sophisticated reasoning and problem-solving skills that the traditional curriculum neglects. These are the skills that adults need in order to select among auto loans, evaluate the health tradeoffs of vaccinating their newborn, or cast an informed vote for a tax referendum. Unlike classroom problems about the speed of a penny dropped from the Eiffel Tower, real-world problems often have murky answers that unfold in complex contexts. Is the tax revenue from a new oil refinery worth the groundwater pollution it creates? Do the financial benefits of buying a house outweigh the convenience of renting? To what extent? What factors could alter the equation? Should I pay an expert to help me decide? Students who learn only the Eiffel Tower version are startlingly unable to take what they've learned and apply it outside the classroom.

"The most damaging evidence against . . . conventional math and science courses," says James Moffett (1994), "comes not from the large numbers of students who failed such courses, scored low on standardized tests, or avoided the courses in the first place, but from the equally large number of students who did *well* in the courses. My wife and I both took four years of math in high school and always got As, but we have not truly integrated math into our lives. We have seldom remembered and applied it when needed, never learned to think mathematically, and never became what math teachers today call mathematically literate. We were temporarily trained monkeys. Most good students who are not especially gifted or interested in math can give the same testimony. High scores merely mask this failure" (pp. 208–209).

A Met advisor says, "I often think about a student at my old school who got good grades in algebra and geometry. I had been her biology teacher. While driving her to college, I found out that she didn't know how to read a map. Neither did anyone in her family, which it turns out was the reason they wanted me to drive her there. She asked me how long the drive would be, so I said 'It's about 100 miles away and we're going about 50 miles an hour. So how many hours will it take?' She had no idea. None. Then I asked her to estimate within 5 hours of the right answer, and she *still* had no idea. In algebra class she had passed tests that required her to know that 'rate times time equals distance,' but in the real world she had no sense of what that formula meant.

"Or the other day, I was helping a Met student with her 10th-grade quantitative reasoning exhibition. For her LTI at the hospital dietary department, she was doing a project on fat calories and fat grams. She had done a chart in Microsoft Excel and had looked at the numbers, but she didn't really understand it. To probe her understanding, I asked 'How many grams does a pencil weigh?' and she said 'What do you mean *weigh*? Pencils aren't made out of fat!' This was a student who had taken 8 years of math before coming to the Met."

Findings from the National Adult Literacy Survey suggest that these incidents are anything but isolated (Steen, 1997). Shown a couple of typical grocery store labels, only 17% of respondents could say which was a better deal: a 16-ounce jar of peanut butter for $1.89 or a 20-ounce jar for $1.99. And only 4% of respondents could calculate the total interest on a 10-year, $10,000 loan with monthly payments of $156.77. (They needed to multiply $156.77 times 120 payments and subtract $10,000.)

Of the five learning goals, quantitative reasoning has been the most difficult for the Met to achieve using interest-based methods. Advisors strive to integrate it into student projects, but this rarely happens to the Met's satisfaction. Most students who develop high-level quantitative skills do so through methods that have much in common with traditional math classes—SAT prep groups, in-school workshops, one-on-one skills tutoring, and college classes.

There are several reasons for this situation. First, the majority of Met students arrive in ninth grade needing remedial work in basic math. Second, the Met's freedom to pursue its own math agenda is limited by the need for students to perform adequately on the state math tests and college entry exams. Third, most Met advisors—like most American college graduates—are less skilled in quantitative reasoning than in the Met's other learning domains. Last, methods for interest-based and project-oriented quantitative learning are still in the earliest stages of development. Dennis and Elliot believe that the school will overcome these obstacles; they've had notable successes with some students, but fewer than they had hoped. In the meantime, they believe that Met students are learning at least as much math as students in conventional schools. Chapter 9 explores this topic further and discusses Met student outcomes on standardized tests.

Empirical Reasoning: How Do I Prove It?

"The idea of the empirical reasoning learning goal," an advisor says, "was to go beyond the endless factoids of conventional biology, chemistry, and physics classes, which most students quickly forget. We want them to develop a scientific thinking process which they can then apply to *any* subject area, and also to daily life. Instead of believing whatever they hear or read, we want them to be able to assess the credibility of different sources and use information wisely to make decisions. In other words, we want them to develop logic skills and a healthy dose of skepticism. So when they argue for positions that aren't based on good evidence, we explore that with them and help them think more logically."

Kiyo's interest in marine biology led to an LTI with the Narragansett Bay Commission. His project was part of an initiative to monitor the bay's water quality in order to guide public policy and raise public awareness. If they find that high phosphate levels correlate with reduced flounder catches, for example, new legislation might regulate fertilizer use by farms in the watershed. To guide his hypotheses, Kiyo studied how pollution, population growth, and the advent of water treatment had affected water quality. His mentor, a biologist, taught him basic lab skills for drawing and analyzing water samples. With the resulting data, Kiyo helped to create a more accurate profile of water quality in the bay.

Met students also apply empirical reasoning to fields outside the traditional bounds of high school science. Brenda did her LTI

with a Providence police officer, and her main project was to help
the department improve relations with teenagers. (She also spent
time in a squad car and responded to everything from domestic
disputes to homicides.) With help from a Brown University sociolo-
gist, she developed a survey and gathered responses from 120
students in high school classrooms. Two of her findings contra-
dicted the police department's prevailing beliefs: First, many students reported *positive* attitudes toward the police; and second,
students reported that their contacts with police occurred more
often in schools and community centers than on the streets. Based
on these findings, Brenda's final report challenged the department's
emphasis on community policing as the best way to improve relations with teenagers. She suggested that the police should increase
their positive presence in schools and community centers instead.

The formal components of the empirical reasoning learning
goal are as follows:

- Developing Strategies to Test Ideas
    Ask questions and pose hypotheses
    Plan creative ways to obtain information
    Design controls, samples, and methods
- Research
    Observation, measurement, data collection, precision
    Find information: print materials, interviews, video,
        Internet
    Understand cause and effect
    Evaluate validity of sources
- Logic
    Interpret data and information
    Reason inductively and deductively
    Explain the logical steps that led to your conclusion

Personal Qualities: What Do I Bring to This Process?

Robert arrived at the Met diagnosed with attention deficit disorder
and a complete inability to organize his work. Sure enough, he
repeatedly lost his journal and mauled his daily planner. He
couldn't manage to hold on to a single piece of work for his portfolio
box. The Met's special-needs director (a vice-principal who wears

many hats) suggested putting a milk crate in the classroom and having Robert just throw his work into it, to be organized later. After several weeks, the crate was empty except for a pair of dirty socks.

Three years later, for his senior project, Robert oversaw the hunger action rally, service day, petition, and fund-raiser described in the previous chapter. "Organizing it has been very complex," his advisor says. "He's got a binder with 20 dividers—budgeting, timelines, correspondence, and so on—and he's managing eight students who are helping with different pieces. He's finally using the strategies we've harped on for so long, because he really *cares* about this project. Suddenly he *needs* a binder and a timeline. But getting responsible and organized hasn't happened overnight. He's taken advantage of a lot of opportunities in between. In 10th grade he organized a rock concert for a local venue, and he had to design, print, and sell tickets, arrange for security, and book the bands. He was totally stressed out, but it was important to him. The hunger project multiplies that complexity by a hundred. He's gone through an amazing transformation."

The fifth learning goal—personal qualities for work, family, and community success—cuts across the other four. The Met has not established a fixed list of required personal qualities, but the ones mentioned most often are persistence, cooperation, organization, leadership, assertiveness, empathy, responsibility, creativity, tolerance, resourcefulness, self-awareness, initiative, respect, persuasiveness, and the ability to plan, prioritize, manage conflicts, and bounce back from setbacks. Traditional schools consider most of these qualities "extracurricular," but at the Met they are central to the curriculum.

When Milan arrived at the Met, he was withdrawn and full of rage. Schoolmates at previous schools had tormented him relentlessly, so at the Met he made a preemptive strike by shunning everyone in his advisory. His computer skills became a weapon for crashing other students' computers and inventing high-tech excuses for neglecting his work.

One day in 10th grade, Milan was being pestered by another student and pretended not to care. Then some invisible line was crossed, and suddenly tiny Milan was chasing huge Lenny around the room with a stapler poised for attack. "He had no intermediate form of communication," his advisor says. "It was either nothing or an all-out explosion. I pulled them aside to mediate, and Lenny was like 'Hey, I was just playing around!'

"'But I didn't *want* him pestering me anymore,' Milan said.

"'Did you tell him that?' I asked.

"'No, I just wanted him to stop.'

"So we had a big discussion about how you need to verbalize what you want. We had several go-rounds like that, and that was when Milan began coming out of his social isolation and trusting the group a little more."

By senior year, Milan had taken on leadership roles in the school and enjoyed teaching younger students how to use computers. Instead of avoiding hard work, he signed up for college classes in statistics and microeconomics. He says that he still feels different from his classmates, but he also feels like an insider because differentness is so common at the Met.

"We have a real intolerance for intolerance here," his advisor says. "We insist on respect, and I think that feeling respected and welcomed was the biggest reason for Milan's huge changes in attitude. At his exit interview, he said something amazing for a kid who had arrived here so determined to shut people out. When we asked him what about the Met had been most important to him, he said it was the close relationships with students in his advisory."

Research on emotional intelligence shows that academic skills mean little in the workplace if an employee lacks personal skills. Once a modest threshold of academic skills has been reached, personal qualities become better predictors of job performance (Murnane & Levy, 1996b). Moreover, high grades and IQ are not the best predictors of career success. Many academic superstars suffer from arrogance, inflexibility, or other qualities that undermine their success, and many low-performing students have superb people skills that lead to superior job performance (Goleman, 1998). The U.S. Secretary of Labor affirmed these findings in the SCANS report (1991), and Goleman (1995) shows that emotional intelligence affects success not only at work but also in personal and civic life.

Creating a precise definition of each personal quality is difficult, as discussed further in Chapter 9. For now, the Met relies heavily on the pragmatic but imprecise "we know it when we see it" approach. The school has also begun to identify the components of some of the personal qualities, as follows:

- Respect
  Respect self, others, and property
- Responsibility
  Complete tasks and be personally accountable
- Leadership
  Positively influence a group
  Plan and facilitate group work
- Organization
  Plan tasks and projects
  Manage time effectively
  Organize materials and work
- Physical Fitness
  Strive for health and fitness
  Understand health and fitness issues
- Perseverance
  Demonstrate commitment to work and goals, despite frustration
- Self-Awareness
  Reflect on one's learning through journals and narrative reports
  Understand and explain one's own emotions and behavior
  Articulate personal interests and goals

Problems with the Learning Goals

The Met's directors are not fully satisfied with how the learning goals have been defined or implemented. "We're trying to make them usable by students," Dennis says, "so why are we using obtuse phrases like 'empirical reasoning?' Instead we sometimes use questions like 'How do I prove it?' That's an improvement, but even those aren't the exact right questions. We need better ways to capture our ideas."

"One problem I have with the learning goals," an advisor adds, "is that sometimes they compartmentalize things in a fake way. Like a student is doing a fashion show, so she studies the chemical structure of polyester fibers even though she has no interest in that. Our mistake is that we're interpreting empirical reasoning too conventionally, which is exactly what we were trying to avoid. We're trying to 'find' the biology, chemistry, or physics in the fashion world. Instead we should be searching for fashion questions that the student finds compelling, such as 'Why are some fashions more popular than others?' Then we could generate a series of hypotheses that could be used to investigate those questions empirically, such as 'The fashion industry actually *creates* people's preferences' or 'Emphasizing certain body parts is advantageous from an evolutionary perspective.'"

"Too often our thinking starts with the learning goals instead of with student interests," Elliot says. "We should start with interest-based projects and then figure out how the learning goals can be achieved through those projects. But sometimes we say, 'This student needs to do more social reasoning,' and then we put together a project or a workshop that doesn't get into the student's interests deeply enough. In those cases, the learning goals become an artificial barrier to getting students to use their minds more rigorously. When we do a better job of adapting the learning goals to student interests, that's when we get more rigor."

Learning Teams and Learning Plans

All high schools strive to cover a vast terrain. Conventional schools bound that terrain with sequences of courses, and they contend that students who pass the courses have fulfilled the school's learning goals well enough to earn a diploma. But that contention seems questionable in many cases, such as the student discussed above who earned good grades in algebra and geometry but couldn't compute the driving time to college.

At the Met, there is no standard sequence of courses. Interest-based projects bound the terrain, so every student achieves the learning goals differently. But pursuing interests does not guarantee that a student will make good decisions about his education. That's why each student has a learning team that includes the student, the advisor, the LTI mentor, parents, and, when appropriate, the special education director. The learning team meets quarterly to create a learning plan for the next quarter. These meetings often take place right after a student's exhibition so that parents and mentors can attend both events during a single visit to the school. Before each learning plan meeting, students must fill out a cover sheet that asks:

> What are your interests and passions?
> What experiences and skills would you like to gain while at the Met?
> What are your goals after the Met?
> What are your strengths?
> What areas do you need to work on?
> How do you learn best? (Describe your learning style.)
> What obstacles have you overcome?

Parents are asked to answer these same these questions about their child, and they provide valuable insights. Asking parents to ponder and specify their goals for their child's education brings them more deeply into the learning process. These are not just token questions that make a pretense of parental influence but are then ignored; parents are essential partners whose input shapes the student's learning activities.

The extent of parent input varies widely. At one learning-plan meeting I attended, the father simply agreed with whatever the advisor proposed. When the advisor asked the father's opinion about several issues, the father had little to say. To help parents develop a stronger voice, the Met recently began offering training sessions on understanding and becoming productively involved in exhibitions and learning-plan meetings.

At the other extreme, one mother offered extensive comments on her son's presentation style and his progress in calculus and computer programming. For the next quarter's learning plan, she pressed for deeper exposure to 17th- to 20th-century history, including specific books to read and strategies for integrating music, art, and philosophy into the historical inquiry. Then she scheduled another learning-team meeting for a month later, rather than waiting until the next quarterly meeting.

The learning plan itself is a full-page grid that students fill out in collaboration with their learning team. Down the side of the grid students list their proposed work for the quarter, and across the top are eight column headings related to that work. One 10th grader planned to do an LTI with the Assembly of God Christian coffeehouse and write a paper about the history of Christian coffeehouses. For that row of his learning plan, the eight columns were filled out as follows:

1. Quantitative Reasoning:
   Create graph showing growth of Pentecostal movement.
2. Communication:
   Write letters and make calls for setting up coffeehouse.
   Read information on the Pentecostal movement.
3. Empirical Reasoning:
   Make plan to get computer operational. Research
      coffeehouses and Pentecostal movement.
4. Social Reasoning
   Citizenship, cooperation, understanding history of the
      Pentecostal movement.
5. Personal Qualities
   Responsibility, organization.
6. What resources will I use?
   Internet, library, church literature.
7. When will I work on it? How will my advisor know?
   During independent work times on MWF. Show drafts
      of paper. Show operational computer.
8. What will I show at my exhibition?
   Paper and LTI summary, work logs, letters written.

Those eight items comprised one row of this student's learning plan. Other rows detailed other planned activities. Some cells were empty, because not every project needs to address every learning goal.

To help the learning team plan the quarter's activities, the Met has developed the following expectations for all students:

Annual Expectations (must be completed every year)

- Follow interests in the real world (informational interviews, job shadows, and LTIs)

- Obtain an LTI during the first semester
- Have a positive impact on the community (service learning, etc.)
- Meet with learning-plan team at least three times per year
- Be aware of gaps in learning and address them through project work
- Create at least four learning plans per year
- Complete the work in the learning plans
- Build a binder of best work and a portfolio of all work
- Have four public exhibitions per year
- Write in journals three times per week
- Schedule daily planners every week
- Come to school on time every day
- Be responsible for actions and locations; sign out of advisory
- Show respect for self and others
- Take responsibility for the learning process
- Take advantage of opportunities
- Make productive summer plans

Met 101 (9th-grade expectations)

- Complete all Annual Expectations
- Do at least one "nested egg" project
- Prepare for the state health assessment
- Read at least three books, and create a reading inventory
- Work on the Quantitative Reasoning areas of Tables and Graphs, Ratios I, and Direct Measurement

Met 201 (10th-grade expectations)

- Complete all Annual Expectations
- Do at least two "nested egg" projects
- Prepare for the state language arts and math assessments
- Read at least five books, and update reading inventory
- Present mini-exhibitions in each learning-goal area during third quarter
- Create a binder of best project work from 9th and 10th grades
- Begin to visit colleges and look at requirements

- Work on the Quantitative Reasoning areas of Linear Models, Ratios II, and Indirect Measurement

Met 301 (11th-grade expectations)

- Complete all Annual Expectations
- Demonstrate heightened personal qualities and depth of work
- Play a leadership role in the school
- Get senior thesis proposal approved by committee
- Read at least six books, including two autobiographies, and update reading inventory
- Write first 25 pages of autobiography
- Work on the Quantitative Reasoning areas of Non-Linear Models, Probability, and Statistics
- Prepare for the state writing assessment
- Meet with college counselor and share information with your learning-plan team
- Research five colleges and their admission requirements
- If gaps remain in college admission requirements, address them in learning plan
- Bring family to college night
- Visit at least three colleges
- Create a draft of college essay
- Begin to create a college portfolio (résumé, transcripts, essay, awards, best work)
- Prepare for and take PSAT in the fall
- Prepare for and take SAT or ACT in the spring
- Schedule at least four college interviews for next year

Met 401 (12th-grade expectations)

- Complete all Annual Expectations
- Demonstrate heightened personal qualities and depth of work
- Play a leadership role in the school
- Meet consistently with senior thesis mentor
- Contact a resource related to the thesis at least every other week and keep track of these contacts

- Complete an in-depth senior thesis project
- Read a book each month (nine total, including one autobiography) and update reading inventory
- Write a 75- to 100-page autobiography
- Prepare for and take the SAT or ACT
- Complete a college portfolio
- Visit and interview with at least four colleges
- Research and apply to colleges
- Apply for scholarships and financial aid
- Create a post-Met plan
- Present work and reflection at graduation exhibition

An important milestone at the Met is entry into Senior Institute, the formal division between the first and second half of high school. At the end of 10th grade, students give two exhibitions to show that they have fulfilled the requirements of Met 101 and 201. In addition to compiling a portfolio of their best work, they must obtain four letters of recommendation (parent, mentor, advisor, and peer), write an essay about their readiness to be promoted, and be interviewed by a panel that assesses their readiness. Students who are not ready must complete summer work specified by their learning team or else repeat 10th grade.

A common critique of Progressive schools is that teachers don't guide student learning enough. Even John Dewey, the most prominent architect of Progressive reform, ridiculed the "tendency in so-called advanced schools of thought . . . to say, in effect, let us surround students with certain materials, tools, appliances, etc., and then let pupils respond to these things according to their own desires. Above all, let us not suggest any end or any plan to the students; let us not suggest to them what they shall do, for that is an unwarranted trespass upon their sacred intellectual individuality. . . . Now such a method is stupid . . . for it misconceives the conditions of independent thinking" (1926/1984, pp. 58–59).

Surely the Met does not resemble Dewey's caricature. Students have abundant latitude to pursue their interests, but they must follow the school's requirements and show adequate progress at quarterly exhibitions. These systems allow the Met to provide guidance and demand accountability while preserving a personalized approach to learning.

7 Standards and Assessment

"We're worried that Jo won't be promoted," her advisor told me just before the exhibition. "It's halfway through the year, and she still hasn't found an LTI. Her motivation hasn't been improving, and her parents aren't pushing her at home or attending her exhibitions. Things aren't going well."

Dennis and a second advisor were already seated in the advisory room, along with three students. Jo's rainbow beads and flowing hair evoked the 60s, but her studied indifference was distinctly 90s. She had already done job shadows at the Wildlife Fund, Urban Solutions, and other nonprofits, but none had sparked her interest.

The Nature Coalition was next, and Dennis applied some pressure: "If you do your LTI there, I need you to work hard. It's a great national group, and we have great connections with them that could last for years. I can't have them bailing out because one student didn't make good on her commitments. Let me know if you take it, because we should sit down and do some planning. And if you *don't* take it, let me know that too, because I'm setting up service learning projects for students who haven't found LTIs yet."

Jo began showing her work from the past quarter. She had retrieved government data and created graphs showing how access to quality health care varied for families of different ethnicities and income levels. She pointed out that, unlike the previous quarter, this time she had completed her main project. But an advisor challenged her: "Can I comment on your level of effort? I think one reason you finished this quarter's project is that it was much easier than last quarter's. You've done a nice set of graphs, but it's not a whole quarter's worth of 10th-grade caliber work."

Next the exhibition panel concluded that Jo had not gone deep enough with several of the tasks on her learning plan. "You can't just *read* the book about Lori Berenson," her advisor said. "You need to do some analysis and writing about why two Peruvian presidents have kept an American human rights journalist in prison for 6 years without a shred of credible evidence against her. Or why two American presidents haven't come to her aid, despite the appalling lack of due process in her trial. We know the answers are in your head, but you need to get them out on paper."

Jo did make some analytic comments later, off the cuff, about the Grateful Dead's attempts to promote community through their music and live shows. "Now *that's* the kind of thinking we're looking for," Dennis said. "These writers and rock bands are trying to get people to *think*. And that's what I just heard you doing for the past 15 seconds."

Then the push for accountability continued. "Have you been reading a lot?" Dennis asked.

"Not that much—I didn't have time," Jo said.

"Too busy doing math problems?" Dennis quipped.

"No, too much time hanging out."

"So what do you need to do?" her advisor asked.

"I need to follow through more."

"This is your sixth exhibition, and you've said that same thing every time. So I need to ask you what concrete actions you're planning to take."

"I suppose I should be more friendly to you. Then we wouldn't have to argue so much."

"I'd really like that. But I must admit that you've said *that* before too. When I sit down to talk with you, it seems like you see that as a punishment."

"I guess I don't like people reminding me of what I need to do."

"But *someone* needs to check your progress every day. Would you get more work done if that was someone other than me? Your mother? A friend?"

Jo nominated a friend, a hard-working senior, and the panel fleshed out a plan for checking her work daily. Next they discussed the sociology course Jo would soon be taking at a local college. "Prove me wrong," Dennis challenged. "If you can't get motivated even to write in your journal, I'm really worried that you won't be able to do the homework for a college course. I get embarrassed when a college gives us a generous scholarship and then our student flunks the course. If it was up to me, I would say don't take the course until you've got your other work back on track. That's our usual policy. But your advisor already agreed to sign you up, so go do it and prove me wrong."

Last they discussed books Jo had read during the past quarter. She talked about loving *The Bell Jar* and *Go Ask Alice* because they had helped her understand problems in her own life. That's when Dennis again turned positive: "See, that's what I've loved about this exhibition—the 40 seconds when you talked about really loving things, because I know you have that specialness inside you. I hear that passion in your voice."

Dennis also praised her carefully organized notebook, which was blanketed with Grateful Dead emblems. Always attentive to student strengths, he asked if she knew the lyrics to all their songs by heart. Jo nodded yes. Dennis looked her right in the eyes, in a way that showed he was impressed. And he wasn't pretending.

How Exhibitions Work

Exhibitions allow students to demonstrate their understanding of what they've learned and to reflect publicly on their growth, their plans, and the problems they need to overcome. They take place at school or at the LTI site, and the audience always includes the advisor and fellow students. Whenever possible, parents, LTI mentors, community members, and additional Met staff also attend the exhibition.

Students begin by handing out their learning plan, a progress report, and a description of their work's importance to themselves, the school, and the LTI site or some other beneficiary. Then they present their work formally, followed by a question-and-answer period and a brainstorming session.

Brainstorming focuses on issues such as "What additional resources could advance your learning?" and "How can we help you grow?" Questions from panelists are designed to assess the depth of students' understanding and their ability to apply what they've learned to new situations. One student had designed a spreadsheet to track hospital volunteers, and a panelist asked why the student hadn't taken the simpler approach of typing the data into a word processor. The student's response made it clear that she didn't understand the advantages of spreadsheets for data management, analysis, and reporting.

In contrast, another student brought a computer to her exhibition and did a live demonstration of the spreadsheet she had developed. When asked what she would do if she needed to incorporate a new variable into her model later, her answer exceeded the panelist's expectations. Rather than just explaining how she would do it, she immediately modified the spreadsheet to include the new variable.

Another role of panelists is to "distribute the nagging," as one advisor said. Panelists comment on students' shortfalls and push them to take more responsibility for their work. When a student's work has been inadequate, the advisor discusses it ahead of time with the learning team. This helps the exhibition move beyond reprimands and focus on solutions.

Shaming is never the goal, but some students do feel ashamed when their shortcomings are discussed publicly or when they see the disappointment of adults they respect. "Margaret barely passed 10th grade," her advisor says, "and then the next quarter she barely lifted a finger. Her exhibition was terrible. As it was ending, another advisor spoke up. 'Are you kidding me? All you have for a whole quarter is one book report and one math ditto? For eight weeks worth of work?'

"The tears slowly welled up in her eyes, and then the whole dam broke. She sobbed and sobbed and felt awful about herself. I was worried, so I called her that night and checked in with her mother. But a couple weeks later she got a great LTI, and she's much different now. She's still immature, but she's gotten more responsible. One school of thought is that students shouldn't do an exhibition if they're unprepared, but in this case it was a turning point. That moment of utter failure and being held to a higher standard set some important changes in motion. It wouldn't have worked with every student, and it wouldn't have worked if she didn't respect us, but it worked. Sometimes you need to cut students slack, and sometimes you need to be painfully honest."

Cramming for an exhibition is impossible, because the Met evaluates both the product and the process. Even a top-notch exhibition would be judged less favorably if the student dawdled all semester and then pulled an all-nighter to prepare. Students must develop good work habits, not just the right answer. The school's smallness allows advisors to monitor work habits and help students improve.

Exhibitions take different forms depending on the student's projects and grade level. Early in ninth grade, students emphasize what they've done to begin exploring their interests. Later in the year, they focus more on LTIs and other projects. The final exhibition of 10th grade focuses on promotion to Senior Institute, and most 12th-grade exhibitions focus on senior projects and post-Met plans.

Less visible than the exhibition itself are the extensive preparation and follow-up that exhibitions require. As with real-world projects, students must anticipate the time needed for each phase of the work and plan accordingly. Students and advisors draft a work schedule at the beginning of each quarter and then confer daily or weekly to assess progress. A few weeks before the exhibition, most advisors hand out a list of expectations and require students to prepare a detailed outline and do a dry run. Students must also write a paper describing their progress during the previous quarter.

Pre-selecting an appropriate panel makes exhibitions more powerful. Advisors choose panelists who care about the student, who will offer support and challenges, and whom the student wants to impress. "Often the best panelists are other students," one advisor said. "If I have a student who needs to be held more accountable, I get upper-class students to help. Younger students look up to them, so their words can have a deeper impact. As for parents, we need to help them have more of a voice. Most of them have never been invited to help plan and evaluate their child's education. This year we had our first training to help parents understand exhibitions and learning plans better and get more involved."

Sometimes panelists are selected because they have expertise relevant to a student's project. "Julia's exhibition on liver cancer research was like a tennis match," her advisor says. "She would explain some complex point, and then her mentor would respond. I'm a science person, but I still had no idea if a particular mouse antibody was secondary or tertiary or whatever. That's when you absolutely need an outside person at the exhibition."

After the exhibition, the learning team decides if the student has fulfilled her learning plan adequately and thereby passed for the quarter. Students who don't pass must do makeup work, usually within 2 weeks. Even when students do pass, parts of their work may be incomplete at the time of the exhibition. If appropriate, those parts are included in the next quarter's learning plan.

Exhibitions are sometimes videotaped, and students are asked to answer questions while reviewing the video: Did you use nervous expressions like "you know" too much? How was your eye contact? Which topics were most difficult to express? When did you speak most clearly? Why do you think this was?

Students also reflect on their exhibition in writing and in meetings with their advisor. Typical questions include: What have you learned about yourself? What problems did you encounter? How did you overcome them? What makes you proud of your work? What would you change to make it better? What advice would you give advisors about preparing students better for exhibitions?

That final question is powerful, because few schools invite students to evaluate teachers. It sends students the message that adults value their opinions, and it models the self-improvement strategies that Met students are encouraged to develop. The question also erodes the illusion of omniscience that some educators promote, an illusion that undermines student-teacher relations and the democratic values professed by American high schools.

The Met does not assign letter grades. Instead, advisors write lengthy narratives each quarter about each student. The bulk of each narrative is a review of the student's exhibition and progress during the past quarter, followed by suggestions for the next quarter or year.

Why Exhibitions and Narratives, Not Tests and Grades?

Exhibitions are often called "authentic" or "performance-based" assessments, because students must demonstrate their mastery of skills and personal qualities that matter in the world outside the school. In response to the limitations of conventional testing, many schools and states have begun to design authentic assessment systems. The Coalition of Essential Schools, which advocates graduation-by-exhibition for all students, has been a pioneer in this effort (MacDonald, Smith, Turner, Finney, & Barton, 1993).

The Met prefers authentic assessment for several reasons. First, assessments at the Met need to be personalized. Every student pursues a unique curriculum, so group tests make no sense. Second, exhibitions are better than conventional tests at assessing a student's understanding of complex issues in relation to real-world contexts. Third, exhibitions transmit the Met's culture from older to younger students.

"You should have seen it," Dennis said. "Here's one of the coolest students in the school talking at his exhibition in this hip but very serious way about all the work he's done: 'Yeah, here's the play I wrote for my senior project. And here's my 75-page autobiography.'

"'*Seventy-five* pages?' a 10th grader gasped.

"'I used to think that was long too, but once you get writing'—snaps his fingers—'seventy-five pages is easy.'"

"So now every student in the room is thinking about autobiographies differently," Dennis said. "Then this cool student talks about the college he got into, his $18,000 financial aid package, and how he's moved from drugs and violence toward getting serious about education. And it's not an *adult* saying it—it's a kid who's been *through* it. It transmits the culture and raises the standards. Now students will start having their senior thesis topic sooner or writing their autobiographies sooner, because they've seen it and they're thinking ahead."

Fourth, exhibitions build skills that conventional tests ignore. "Danny could sit down and get all the answers right on a test," his advisor says. "But that wouldn't help him with his central problem, which is getting organized. Exhibitions force him to work on that. He needs to develop an outline and an agenda, prepare handouts, assemble a work portfolio, rehearse, and make a well-organized presentation. We evaluate him on the organization of his work in addition to the actual content of what he learned."

Then there are the inherent limitations of tests and letter grades. In *The Schools Our Children Deserve*, Alfie Kohn (1999) reviews a mountain of research on this topic. He concludes that tests and grades promote low-level skills and temporary retention of facts, but they work against long-term retention of facts and the development of high-level skills, deep understanding of ideas, and motivation to learn.

How do tests and grades thwart these important goals (all of which are central to the reform agendas of mainstream American schools)? Kohn's (1999) research yields several answers. First, tests tend to focus on small questions that have clear-cut answers. These tests are easy to grade, but they don't require students to show deep understanding of what they've learned and the ability to apply it outside the classroom.

Second, tests and grades often reflect an overemphasis on achievement. This backfires by rewarding students for avoiding challenges that might lower their grades. "A school that constantly emphasizes . . . performance! results! achievement! success!" Kohn (1999) says, may produce children who "find it difficult to get swept away with the process of creating a poem, trying to build a working telescope, or figuring out why fighting always seems to be breaking out in the Balkans. . . . Students who have put success out of their minds . . . process information more deeply, review things they didn't understand the first time, make connections between what they're doing now and what they learned earlier, and use more strategies to make sense of the ideas they're encountering" (pp. 27, 31).

Third, grades are useful for ranking students, but ranking teaches students to compete rather than cooperate, and to judge their own competence in relation to defeating others. Lower-ranked students are not the only ones harmed by this mindframe. "No matter how well you do at the Met," an advisor says, "your learning team will always point out something you need to work on. That's very different from getting an A, which in some ways puts an upper bound on what you're expected to learn. For students who have always earned top grades, suddenly the pressure is on because now they're competing with themselves. They're always trying to outdo their last exhibition."

Grades and test scores also offer a false sense of objectivity and precision. Assigning an essay grade of 87 or 92 is like eyeballing someone from across the room and then confidently reporting that he weighs 143 pounds. Two students who earn a B+ in American

Literature could differ vastly in skills and knowledge, depending on which school they attend and which teacher grades their assignments. Even multiple-choice tests such as the SAT and many state exams are less objective than they seem. Susan Ohanian (1999) and David Owen (1999) offer several examples of students whose deep thinking revealed correct responses other than the one endorsed by the test maker. Often those students' answers are marked wrong anyway, a practice that penalizes students for thinking beyond the obvious (but incorrect) answer.

The bottom line is that assessments should predict how well students will do on important future tasks. But Kohn (1999) cites a synthesis of 35 studies showing that grades and test scores are poor predictors of future job effectiveness.

By overemphasizing grades and test scores, schools have lost sight of the most important reason for evaluating student work: to help students learn. A terse D or F on a report card says nothing about how a student could improve his work. The Met's narrative evaluations paint a more informative and forward-looking picture:

"It was very difficult for Tanya to motivate herself to finish her papers on time," one advisor wrote. "She left them until the last minute, which made it impossible for me to give her adequate feedback. Tanya has a lot of raw talent as a writer. She wrote an editorial on campaign finance reform that was the best in our advisory. If she would leave herself the time to really edit and perfect a piece of writing, she could become a truly outstanding writer." This rich detail continued for three pages.

In contrast, a suburban high school near Providence scrunches mid-quarter student evaluation onto a 3-by-5 index card. Teachers are required to check off one or more pre-printed problems and solutions, such as "Receives unsatisfactory grades" and "Spend more time on work." If the teacher wants to elaborate, there is a comments section roughly the size of two postage stamps. A stiff directive at the bottom says, "If conference is desired, call guidance office for an appointment"—and the phone number isn't included. With responsibility for more than 100 students, teachers have little choice but to write meager comments and direct parents to a guidance counselor who barely knows their child.

Most students come to the Met from large public schools, and their parents lament the minimal feedback they have received in the past. They appreciate the Met's detailed and personalized narratives, which reflect a curriculum that the parents helped design, meetings that the parents attended, and a teacher whom the parents know well.

But exhibitions and narratives also present formidable challenges. Tests are easy to administer and grade, but exhibitions are messy and complicated. They require flexible scheduling, rehearsals, and group consensus about the quality of students' work. Panelists need the confidence and know-how to offer support and ask probing questions. Advisors must assemble appropriate panels, orchestrate productive exhibitions, and write lengthy narratives that offer learning suggestions while carefully balancing praise with constructive criticism. The Met's staff accept these challenges, because they believe that exhibitions and narratives lead to superior learning.

Standards One Student at a Time

"Clear outcomes are on every list of what makes a great school," Dennis says. "But we need to look at that notion more closely. The Met believes strongly in setting specific *short-term* outcomes, namely each student's learning plan, but our *long-term* outcomes are very flexible. We revisit learning plans every quarter, so if a student gets particularly interested in a new topic, she can move in that direction.

"We decide on outcomes one student at a time, because our learning goals set high standards but allow tremendous latitude across students. For our student who was in drug rehab, we had very specific requirements because we weren't there every day to look over her shoulder. But look at Tamika, one of our huge success stories. Who could have ever guessed that she was going to start a very successful nonprofit organization? If we had set clear long-term outcomes for her up front, we would have missed her potential. She never would have shot for the stars.

"In that sense, our school is more like life than most schools. Many adults have a general sense of what they want in life, but at the outset they don't know exactly how they're going to get there. They feel their way through, looking for the best opportunities with the best people. That's what we do at the Met. We believe that putting students in great environments will lead to the best outcomes for each student, one student at a time."

"The diploma should mean that a student is excited about learning," Elliot adds, "not just that he's learned some fixed body of knowledge. Mastering a curriculum but thinking it's boring and losing interest in learning is not the answer. With the information explosion, our job is to make sure that students *want* to get information and know how to get it and use it. Most schools just want to know if a student *can* read. We want to make sure that they *do* read now and in the future. That's why our standards are so complicated."

The Met collides head-on with America's sprint toward uniform standards, whose main impetus is a belief that inferior schools are crippling our economic competitiveness. The mainstream standards process involves defining what constitutes a well-educated student, designing tests to measure progress toward that standard, and then giving rewards (e.g., higher teacher salaries) or imposing sanctions (e.g., withholding diplomas) based on student test scores. These uniform standards are nominally intended to increase motivation, level the playing field for disadvantaged students, and permit judgments of school quality.

In one respect, the standards movement has been an indisputable success: 49 states have adopted statewide standards, and 30 states (not including Rhode Island) have adopted "high-stakes" tests that students must pass in order to graduate. In all other respects, the movement's success has been widely disputed. Parents, educators, advocacy groups, and academics have generated an avalanche of caveats and criticisms that are summarized in recent books by Alfie Kohn (1999), Deborah Meier (2000), the National Research Council (1999), Susan Ohanian (1999), and others. The next two paragraphs are a drastically abridged synthesis of their main points.

Historians have amply refuted the popular myth that American education deteriorated and lost international standing during recent decades. And *everyone* embraces high standards, but the tougher question is who gets to decide what the standards should be. In a democratic society, standards should be defined locally by parents and educators, not at the state or national level. The curriculum frameworks that many states have adopted are laundry lists of rapidly forgotten facts that erode children's enthusiasm for learning. Few adults know—or care to know—these facts by heart. One extensive study concluded that mastering all of them would require even the brightest students to spend more than a decade in high school (Marzano, Kendall, & Gaddy, 1999).

Like taking the temperature of a burning house, the state exams reveal mostly what we already know. Rather than leveling the playing field, they tilt it even more steeply. Schools in middle-class districts squander little time on test preparation, freeing students for higher-level academic pursuits. But the poorest schools focus heavily on tests in order to avoid sanctions. Rather than taking on the great challenges of science and literature, students in these schools waste long hours learning how to fill in bubble sheets and outsmart trick questions. This "teaching to the test" demoralizes teachers and distorts the test results so thoroughly that higher scores might signify little more than improved test-taking skills. Even the multibillion dollar test-making industry insists that low test scores alone are an inadequate criterion for withholding a diploma, yet many states do just that.

"I know that states need to hold schools accountable in some way," Dennis says. "I'm not asking to be excused from that. What I disagree with is having only one way of evaluating each student. Every state says they want students to become good thinkers, problem solvers, and citizens, but then the tests they give have almost nothing to do with those things! Every school should be able to devise its own way of showing that students are achieving what the state claims to value. The Met's exhibitions and portfolios would be satisfactory under that kind of system. We could videotape every exhibition, and the state could randomly select and assess a sample of them."

A unique aspect of the Met's standards is that they assess personal qualities—the fifth learning goal. "Getting promoted to Senior Institute is about being a functional young adult," an advisor says. "If I still need to chase you to do your work, then you're not ready for Senior Institute. It's not just about history and physics; it's about time management, motivation, self-direction, perseverance, and seriousness of purpose. The same is true of our standards for graduation. We need to feel that students can negotiate their own learning more independently than before. Over time they are expected to take on more and more responsibility for their own learning."

Then how much responsibility is enough? How much motivation? What levels of reading and math? "We refuse to set a specific content standard," Elliot says, "because every student starts at a different place. We do it one student at a time, based on their learning plans. You need to have different ways of setting high standards for different students. A test is not a high enough standard. *Using* knowledge—grappling with real problems and real people—that's the *real* test."

"Uniform standards are a myth," Dennis adds. "*All* high schools have different standards for different students. Students who do lower-quality work get tracked into lower-level classes. Then they graduate with lower-quality work but the same grades and credits as someone else. But all of that is beside the point. What's important is that a student learns to work hard and struggle and improve. It's the desire and the effort to improve that's important. If a student moves from the third-grade level to the fifth-grade level, that's great. If a student starts at the tenth-grade level but doesn't move, that's not so great. We do it one student at a time, and they need to show movement.

"Do we require a minimum proficiency level? I'd like to say that we wouldn't graduate a student with a sixth-grade reading level. But on the other hand, there aren't even any measures that assess reading ability very well. Students read and write better when they're interested in the topic, and most of those tests aren't very interesting. If a student is reading at a sixth-grade level even though he's working with his interests and has our great support, then he probably has a learning disability. Then he'll get an individualized education plan, which has its own unique set of standards and graduation requirements anyway. That's the law for all American public schools.

"The flip side of the question is whether students can graduate *sooner* than 4 years if they're ready. Definitely yes, although I'd rather have them stay for the full 4 years. What's the rush? We can offer pretty much anything to our students for the last year of high school. Right now two of our seniors are going to college full time, but we support and guide them a little bit. We have two other students who are spending a year in Japan and Argentina. All of them still have learning plans and need to do exhibitions to graduate. I believe in our environment and our support, and I worry that they'll have less support when they leave here. So I have no problem keeping them here for 4 years."

"In the end," Elliot says, "we base our decisions on a consensus among people who know the student well. *They* are the ones who decide if a student should graduate or pass an exhibition. The decision mostly rests with the advisor, who is in the best position to see the big picture of a student's learning. But if there's disagreement, then we all sit around and discuss it—student, parent, mentor, advisor, and principal."

Local standards sound radical in light of current demands for uniform accountability at the state level, but three of America's most prominent educators speak in favor of them. Howard Gardner says, "Standards are the key to progressive education. . . . Yet they cannot be imposed from without. They must arise naturally, as students and teachers work together over time in an atmosphere of mutual respect" (1991, p. 195).

Herb Kohl (1998) argues that educational experts insist on using standardized tests, no matter how biased and invalid, because they are afraid of local control and don't trust communities to build a system of education that works best for themselves.

And Deborah Meier says, "Local empowerment can often be vicious and retrograde, but so too can nationally imposed power. . . . When it comes to schools, I think the benefits of greater autonomy and local control outweigh the dangers" (2000, p. 83). She believes that the demands of employers and universities will prevent local standards from straying too far afield. Her greater concern is that most schools will not stray far enough.

Schools that want to create local standards often develop careful descriptions of their expectations for student work, known as rubrics. Table 7.1 shows a rubric that one such school uses to rate how well students have organized an essay.

"The good thing about well-constructed rubrics," Elliot says, "is that they get past the sweeping generalizations about student work that are so common in education. Good rubrics help you break down behaviors into their component parts. For example,

Table 7.1: Rubric for Assessing Essays

Level of Organizational Quality	*Assessment*
Uses advanced organizing techniques	A or "Exceeds Standards"
Progresses in an organized way	B or "Meets Standards"
Shows some problems with organization	C or "Approaches Standards"
Shows weak and/or random organization	D or "Just Beginning"

it's not very helpful just to say that a student is disorganized and then stop there. You have to look closer and realize that he's planning his day well but then failing to follow through. The same is true of communication. If you only look at grammar and vocabulary, you miss vital pieces like a student's ability to speak with confidence and conviction."

"The problem with rubrics," Dennis adds, "is that you get caught up in putting check marks on stuff. You lose the total picture. We looked at one school whose rubrics had 800 different parts. It gets in the way of a student getting excited and doing great. In the end, even with rubrics, someone *still* has to make a series of very subjective decisions, such as whether an essay is organized at an 'average' or 'advanced' level. And calling something 'advanced' means something very different depending what classroom, school, or district you're in. Here is that school's rubric for listening skills:

1. Chooses listening strategies appropriate to the material
2. Listens attentively without creating distractions
3. Responds appropriately to the form and content of what is heard
4. Shows few errors in understanding the main ideas—

and that's just half of one section! It's not that I disagree with the 800 criteria, it's just that slogging through all of them for every student isn't the best use of our time. What I'd love is for our teachers to *internalize* these rubrics so they can get a handle on the different pieces of different skills and help students work on them. That's where rubrics can be really helpful."

The Met's reliance on local consensus rather than explicit standards could give the impression of leniency. Countering that impression is the fact that 13 out of 50 10th graders (26%) were not promoted in a recent year. All were required to attend the Met's summer school, except for one student whose summer Outward Bound scholarship was deemed equally beneficial. Then in September the students had to do exhibitions showing that they had completed their summer work satisfactorily. Ten of the 13 students were promoted to 11th grade at that point. By January, each of the remaining three students had completed enough makeup work to be promoted.

The Met's local standards might also be charged with promoting inequity. Diane Ravitch, an educational historian, has said that state or national standards are needed because "the alternative is to go back to a no-standards regime where the wealthy take care of themselves and the poor are left to take the hindmost. . . . The kids who have nothing get nothing . . . and the inequities become multiplied" (in McGrath, 2000). Her concerns are vitally important, and high standards for all students are indeed an essential factor in breaking the cycle of disadvantage. But the Met—a school in which local standards lead to high achievement by low-income students—offers an exception to Ravitch's rule. Rather than relying on state or national standards, with their many shortcomings, the Met offers an alternative approach to fighting inequity in public education.

Not all Met students find it possible or desirable to meet the school's standards, however. Students have been expelled because they wouldn't do enough work, were absent too often, or were too disruptive. But the Met detests losing students and goes to great lengths to accommodate special situations. "We push like crazy on many fronts," Dennis says, "but it's counterproductive to push certain things when it just means that you're going to lose the student. It might sound soft, but it's realistic. We want them to finish school."

"Some students won't demonstrate proficiency in all academic areas during their years in school," Elliot adds. "I know, because I was one of them. Does that mean we pull the plug on them? If we deny them a chance for a diploma, that kills most of their options in life. If we can get them working on something passionately—or even just diligently—then we want to keep them here. We always push students toward challenges, but we stay away from things that are self-defeating and impossible. Our strong preference is for all students to achieve all of the learning goals—and most do—but some of them won't until later in life. Instead of cutting them loose, we can still help them learn other things that they need to know."

Another potential risk of individualized standards is tracking students into pathways that are below their potential, but this does not seem to be a problem at the Met. "Some schools assess you once at the beginning, and then you're pretty much tracked forever," an advisor says. "After Lenny got tested in middle school, he felt that the teachers didn't think he could do much of anything. The Met is the opposite of that. We understood that Lenny had some learning problems, but that didn't stop us from pushing him hard and engaging his passions. One day he said, 'I want to take a college writing class,' and we said, 'Go for it.' He worked really hard and got a B in the course. It was an amazing experience for someone who had been told that he couldn't even succeed in a regular *high school* class. He also learned an important lesson about taking advantage of opportunities. The Met has a powerful culture of hope and success and going after things. At most schools it takes a ton of energy to do anything innovative, because it's so rare. But at the Met everyone's doing creative things, so students who *don't* take initiative end up feeling like slackers."

The standards that Met staff value most are the ones that students develop within themselves. "We want students to be lifelong learners and good citizens," an advisor says. "And when you're an adult, who gives you the standards? *You* do! So it's incredibly important to develop high *internal* standards. The seniors in my advisory surprised me recently by saying that their work has gone downhill over time. 'What do you mean?' I asked them. 'Do you feel like your writing has gotten worse?'

"'No, we're much better writers than before.'

"'Do you think your projects are worse?'

"'No, our projects are much better too, but we used to feel much better about them.'

"And so on. So I suggested that they look back at the early work in their portfolios, and they realized that their work has actually gotten much *better* over time. But back in freshman year they were like 'I finished a project, I'm so great, yippee for me!' Now they say things like 'If I had managed my time better, I could have done this whole other part I was hoping to do.' It's not that their work has gone downhill, it's that their standards for themselves have gotten so much higher."

8 Putting It All Together

It's the stuff no one sees that makes all the difference.

—Dennis Littky

The Met has much in common with America's most effective social programs. "Successful programs create an organizational culture that is . . . tight about their mission but loose about how the mission is carried out. Those responsible for these programs have no illusion that they can implement the perfect model program—at once or ever. They evolve in response to changing needs . . . and feedback from both front-line staff and participants . . . learning from their successes and failures, and finding new and better ways to achieve their goals" (Schorr, 1997, pp. 8–9).

This describes the Met in a nutshell. The school's mission is tight, but its flexibility and resourcefulness are unlimited. Spend a year studying in Argentina? Design stained-glass windows for the new campus? Turn your drug rehab into your internship? Take seven college classes? Absolutely, as long as you're working effectively toward the five learning goals.

The same is true of the Met's flexible roles for people. Everything is subject to scrutiny and redesign. Parents help to plan and assess their child's learning. The office staff serve as mentors and tutors. Students teach students and work with adults outside the school. Community members visit the school often to share their knowledge.

The headline of the Met's teacher recruitment poster is "Are you brave, bold, passionate, and creative?" The school wants teachers with good academic skills, but they emphasize a commodity that's been harder for them to find—the right personal characteristics for Met-style teaching. Foremost is a love of learning and a willingness to work with passion, persistence, and creativity in service of every student's learning.

The ambitious job description has not discouraged applicants, however; each spring the Met has received at least 30 applications for every open position. Applicants often ask if Met staff have time for a personal life, and the answer is yes. A few staff members choose to devote most of their waking hours to their work, but most strike a balance between work and personal life. The Met has hired new and experienced teachers from age 22 to 48, many with children (including two single parents).

The Met's teachers are 76% White, 12% Latino, 6% African-American, and 6% Asian-American. The school actively recruits minority teachers, but the tremendous disparity between teacher and student ethnicity reflects the demographics of certified teachers nationwide. Rhode Island has 4% minority teachers but 25% minority students. The Met, with 24% minority teachers, exceeds every other district in the state (Rhode Island Department of Education, 2000a, 2000b). Still, Dennis isn't satisfied. "Our numbers look good, but we're still bad," he says. The Met is committed to further broadening the diversity of its teachers.

"What suggests to me more than anything that this is a good way to do education," one advisor said, "is that *I've* learned so much more here at the Met than in my own high school and college classes. Our teaching is so hands-on and exciting that I've learned a tremendous amount even in my specialty, which is science. I just met with a student who's interested in catapults, so now I'm figuring out the math and physics behind catapults. Another student is working on stereo stuff, so I'm learning about electricity. I'm really liking it because I'm excited to teach it to the students."

As with any demanding profession, becoming a successful Met advisor is a gradual evolution. New advisors arrive with vulnerabilities, knowledge gaps, and hot buttons. They are plunged into unfamiliar territory and must quickly develop skills that conventional teacher training programs ignore. They don't need to be experts in all subject areas, but they must be willing to be generalists. They have to facilitate student work in all areas and consult with specialists as needed.

One advisor said, "We have the freedom to do whatever works, whenever we can pull it off." But with that freedom comes the expectation that advisors will go to great lengths to succeed with all students. They are expected to hang in there even with students who defy authority, hurl insults, space out, stay home, lack project ideas, need endless nudging, and unravel the best-laid plans—and many Met advisors enjoy the challenge.

To keep pace with so many demands, the Met devotes an exceptional amount of resources to planning and staff development. There are three staff meetings per week, a weekly staff newsletter, a monthly one-day retreat, a monthly book group, visits from consultants, and two planning weeks during the summer. First-year advisors have an additional orientation week. A mentoring system pairs old and new advisors, and the principals touch base individually with each advisor weekly or more often. The Met spends about 12% of its budget on these activities, compared with 2% in other Rhode Island schools. Some of that money comes from grants, not from the Met's public school budget.

"The best staff development is just being part of our school and gradually absorbing what happens here," Dennis says. "During one of our summer planning weeks, I floated a new idea and then broke staff into groups to discuss it. One of our seasoned teachers said, 'I think that's a *terrible* idea!' So I sat down with his group and we had a good conversation about it. A new teacher was shocked at how the other teacher had disagreed so outspokenly with my idea—the principal's idea. But the new teacher quickly learned that the Met culture is to speak your mind and disagree if you want. To work well, our culture needs staff who have thoughtful ideas and opinions on a regular basis."

Also essential are leaders who aren't threatened by those ideas. "One thing I love about our school," an advisor said, "is that I am respected. Neither Doc nor Elliot has ever belittled me or spoken to me in a demeaning, condescending, or patronizing way. Nor have I ever heard them do so to any staff member or student. At age 50, I can tell you that this is extremely rare in the working world. I feel reasonably free to try following my own ideas with students, and having that voice really counts."

The Met's leadership makes such rarities commonplace. Most schools (and other public institutions) are inertial and avoid risks, but not the Met. "Problems are my friends," Dennis says. "That's my mantra if I get bummed out about something. So I breathe deep and remind myself that if school reform was easy, I'd be doing something else. Solving problems is what I'm good at, so let's come up with something better. Part of being a good principal is rolling with the punches, figuring out solutions, and modeling that for others. I've seen over and over again that people can learn that frame of mind. Not just teachers, but students too. A big part of it is mentorship—being with someone over time who is always solving problems. That way people learn that changing things is really possible."

From its inception, the Met has taken risk after risk and tackled problem after problem. Dennis and Elliot refuse to accept the snail's pace of mainstream reform, knowing that it shortchanges the students who will be long gone by the time a 10-year plan has been carried out. They also know that, with so many constituencies to satisfy, the Met's window of opportunity could slam shut if they don't move quickly.

In the early days, when the Met was still being designed, Dennis, Elliot, and the staff of The Big Picture Company developed numerous alliances with state and local government, industry, educators, and community groups. The resulting coalition provided the breathing room (and the eager parents) that enabled the Met to propose sweeping innovations and hold off powerful opponents until the first graduating class provided hard evidence—a 100% college-acceptance rate, among other indicators—that the model deserved serious consideration and continued funding.

Rarely satisfied, the Met often scrutinizes and refines its practices. The school is reluctant to delay action until "proven" alternatives are available, because proof is in short supply in the field of education. Instead, the staff make frequent midcourse corrections. "If you seriously want to improve a school," Dennis says, "the most important thing is developing a culture of evaluation and change. You need to be able to try things and then change or discard them based on experience. I don't believe in adopting some canned method that's reassuring but that you're wedded to whether it's helping or not."

The Met's culture of evaluation includes people too. Dennis and Elliot write lengthy evaluations of each staff member and, unlike many principals, request evaluations of themselves in return. The apparent honesty of the staff's evaluations—mostly positive, but with some pointed criticisms—suggests that Dennis and Elliot have created a rare climate of genuine, two-way communication. Many comments reflected the Met's emphasis on creating a warm and supportive climate for staff.

"Strong relationships are essential in any school," Elliot says, "but that's even more true in a small, personalized school. Our teachers are not behind closed doors in separate classrooms. They work together a lot, so they need to get along and understand each other and care about each other. If teachers are going to model warmth, respect, growth, and support for their students, they need a work environment that provides all those things for staff too."

The Met's warmth is partly a by-product of the staff's shared vision, but it also springs from deliberate attempts at building community. The monthly staff retreats are devoted to work but also include lots of levity. One time Dennis and Elliot brought a masseuse who gave everyone a 15-minute massage. Another time they began by having each staff member thank three others for favors and strengths and jobs well done. "It was so healthy and beautiful," Dennis said, "because we're not a thankful society. We take each other too much for granted. It only took 20 minutes, but it was so powerful."

Shortly after I began my research at the Met, I received a staff roster in my mailbox, with instructions to write something I appreciated about each person on the list. All staff completed one of these sheets, the responses were collated, and then everyone received a beautifully printed page that began "This is what your fellow staff members appreciate about you." I began to see the power of the Met's community-building efforts, because the comments I received made me feel welcome. I was touched to be included even though I was an external researcher, not a staff member.

That same week, just before winter break, Dennis's weekly note in the staff memo featured a big furry Santa Claus face and a note saying "I feel very lucky to be working at the Met. Take a look around at who you work with and the possible growth every day. We can do anything we want to help our kids become outstanding human beings. Thank you all for making my life fun and worthwhile. I love you all. Dennis."

In an article Dennis wrote with Robert Fried, he summarizes all of this in two words—caring and conviviality:

> Caring. What a school is depends more on how people treat each other than on anything else. No slogan, no software, no shortcut can conjure up this most basic of values. That old adage "relationship first, task second" applies equally to a classroom or a committee.
>
> Conviviality. It's all very well to articulate a philosophy of school reform and pursue it in a focused and committed way. But somebody's got to buy the pizzas, bring in the birthday balloons, spice up faculty meetings with fancy pastry and lousy jokes. Conviviality is the quality of acceptance, of geniality and good-naturedness, of creating a culture where people are known and valued for who they are, not just the work they do. (1988, p. 8)

Coexisting with the Met's warmth is a hard-nosed determination to excel as a school and a movement. "Dennis Upgraded to Hurricane Status" was a 1999 news headline, and as the season's fourth tropical storm pounded Cape Hatteras, it bore a certain resemblance to its namesake at the Met—powerful, relentless, expansive, and a bit unpredictable. These qualities are more typically associated with CEOs than with high school principals, but Dennis and Elliot believe that successful schools must utilize strategies that are usually ignored or even spurned in the public sector. In short, they must be entrepreneurial.

The Met and The Big Picture Company devote considerable time to fund raising and public relations, developing a market niche for their unconventional products, and building strategic partnerships with individuals and organizations in Rhode Island and across the country. They have launched several initiatives to disseminate their learning models, including a K–8 charter school in Rhode Island and a national training program for high school principals. Recently they received a $3.4 million grant from the Bill and Melinda Gates Foundation to open 12 Big Picture schools across the country.

Like fledgling corporations, the Met and The Big Picture Company have often adopted a swashbuckling, go-for-broke approach that risked outright failure and groped toward lofty goals in the absence of a well-marked pathway. Their tactics were motivated not by recklessness or thrill-seeking, but by the urgency of their mission and a belief that moving at full force was the only way to break through the barriers.

Now that the Met has established a track record of solid student success, brief as it is, the school is on firmer political ground for implementing a more orderly long-term plan. Yet the staff still want to retain their ability to shift gears when unanticipated opportunities arise. One staff member called this "designing for serendipity"—organizing the school to accommodate the best of whatever they can create, whenever it happens.

Corporate analogies have limitations, of course. The Met's bottom line is not money, and the CEOs are not seeking the biggest slice. In fact, Dennis and Elliot often fund special projects out of their own pockets and on many occasions have helped students with money for clothes, food, or other needs. I've seen Elliot pick up trash as he walks around campus, not worrying that it's somehow beneath his status as principal. He likes nothing better than driving a student home after a school dance and having a long talk at curbside. When Dennis talks about his students' blossoming into young adulthood, he says, "I'm getting that excited feeling in my stomach" and then chokes up and can't finish what he was saying.

Dennis and Elliot often say that they're "in the business of saving children"—a phrase that could sound vain or melodramatic if it weren't so obviously true. During 2 years of close contact with them, I have seen that power and prestige are not why they have become high rollers in the school reform game. They both enjoy a challenge and a slap on the back, but it's clear that helping students is their greatest reward.

9 Does It Work?

"We're definitely preparing our students for life," Dennis says. "The next few years will show if we've also prepared them for college. I'm dying to see how they do. I read somewhere that only 7% of low-income students of color graduate from college within 5 years after high school. Seven percent! It seems way too low to be true, but that's what I read. I *know* we're going to do better than that. But I want to do *way* better than that."

The Gold Standard

Before examining actual data on the Met's effectiveness, it's useful to imagine the perfect evaluation—what professional evaluators call the "gold standard." Most evaluations of schools look at scores on standardized tests, but the Met believes that those tests fail to measure many important outcomes. The first step of the gold standard evaluation is therefore to define the outcomes that the Met *does* consider important. For example, students are expected to become resourceful in tracking down information needed for their projects. Dozens of other desired outcomes are listed in Chapter 7.

Next the evaluators have to find ways to measure those outcomes. Researchers are developing new types of assessments, but the process is expensive and technically demanding. Consider the challenge of measuring an outcome such as resourcefulness. What does an 8th-grade level of resourcefulness look like? How is a 12th-grade level different? What should be the minimum level required for graduation? How often must a student demonstrate it? The complexity of these questions helps to explain why our education system prefers simple (but superficial) grades like B+ or 88%.

Once the evaluators have developed top-notch measures of the Met's learning goals, they need to hold a lottery. They put the names of all Met applicants into a hat and randomly select 200 of them. The first 100 attend the Met, and the second 100 attend other high schools. Then, using the gold standard measures they have just developed, they assess both groups several times over a period of 10 or 20 years. The study is long-term because the Met's most important outcomes are long-term: lifelong intellectual habits, active citizenship, and successful personal and professional lives. By using a lottery to make school assignments, the evaluators have maximized the likelihood that any differences they find later between the two groups can be attributed to the high school they attended.

That takes care of the outcome evaluation. But they also have to do a process evaluation, which attempts to figure out and explain what's actually happening at the school on a day-to-day basis. They would assign researchers to observe each of the Met's components for a year or two and then provide detailed documentation for anyone who wanted to create a school based on similar principles. Without that information, no one could replicate the school's design even if it was successful, because no one would know what the Met actually did to achieve success.

The Real-World Standard

Ranchers who want hefty cows spend more time feeding them than weighing them. Most schools follow that same logic. They are designed as schools, not research projects, so data collection is not the top priority. Less than 1% of all education studies are randomized experiments (Nave, Miech, & Mosteller, 1998), mostly because gold standard studies have golden price tags. Indeed, the Met is currently designing an extensive evaluation that, if funded, will last 10 years and cost $1 million.

Achieving the gold standard is almost impossible, but Lisbeth Schorr and Daniel Yankelovich (2000) call for new forms of evaluation. They emphasize that the traditional gold standard was designed for the field of medicine, which needs "pill versus placebo" research designs that miss the essence of many social programs.

They argue that "the most promising social programs are sprawling efforts with multiple components requiring constant mid-course corrections and flexible adaptation to local circumstances. Because such initiatives don't lend themselves to 'one person getting the pill, the other the placebo,' many evaluators reject them as 'merely anecdotal' or the work of 'charismatic leaders.' . . . Insistence on irrefutable scientific proof . . . has become an obstacle to finding what works, frustrating the nation's hunger for evidence that social programs are on the right path. Ironically, the methods considered most 'scientific' can actually defeat thoughtful assessments of promising interventions" (p. A15).

In short, evaluating the Met's initial effectiveness does not require a gold standard study. Ample evidence already exists, and the following pages provide an overview of that evidence. Like any overview, it inevitably masks some of the complexity of its subject. Earlier chapters capture that complexity more fully, providing an essential backdrop for interpreting this overview accurately. Additional perspectives on the Met's effectiveness and its first class of graduates can be found in a forthcoming publication by Adria Steinberg (in press).

Who and What Are We Evaluating?

The Met's student body is 41% White, 38% Latino, 18% African-American, and 3% Asian-American. Forty-eight percent qualify for free or reduced-price lunch because of low family income. Seventy-five percent live in Providence, and the rest commute from 16 other Rhode Island towns and cities. Only one quarter of the parents have a bachelor's degree, but this group includes parents with advanced degrees, middle-class incomes, and white-collar jobs. The Met now has 200 students and will grow to 700 once the campus is fully constructed.

The Met's effectiveness would be easiest to understand in relation to other high schools with similar students. Unfortunately, there aren't any. The Met has a different composition from other Providence public high schools, because it appeals to such a wide range of students and parents. On key dimensions such as family income and parent-education level, it falls in between the prestigious college-prep magnet school and the other city high schools, although much closer to the latter.

Other features also make the Met's student body unique, although it is unclear whether those features help or hurt student outcomes. For example, the Met's first class signed on to attend a school that didn't have a track record, final approval from the legislature, or even a building to meet in. What can we infer about students and families who would cast their lot with a school whose existence was that tenuous? Were they confident or desperate? Well-informed or apathetic? And what about the students who commute to the Met from the suburbs? Do they want a greater challenge than their local school provides, or were they expelled for unruly behavior? Then there is the parental effort required to complete the Met's application process. (A parent or sponsor must fill out a brief application, attend an interview, and sign an agreement to attend quarterly exhibitions and learning plan meetings.) Do parents do it because they are resourceful and energetic, or because they see the Met as the last hope for a troubled child?

In short, did the Met select only the most promising students and reject the rest? Available evidence points strongly in the opposite direction. First, most of the Met's recruitment takes place in the middle schools that serve the lowest-income residents of Providence. Second, the Met accepted nearly every applicant during its early years, because applications barely exceeded openings. Third, the average ninth grader entering the Met has reading and math skills at the level of a mid-year sixth grader. Fourth, nearly half of the Met's students missed a month or more of school in the year before they arrived, and 10% missed 2 months or more. Students who miss that much school are rarely the most successful ones. Finally, a high proportion of Met students have backgrounds that include severe hardships of many kinds.

Then there's the question of whether we're evaluating the "true" Met model. Every year the Met has added a new grade, transitioned to a new kind of building, or expanded its student body, and the school's main buildings are still under construction. What is the impact of being a new and special school? Once the Met model expanded to dozens of schools and districts, perhaps the feeling of specialness would disappear and take student out-

comes with it. Conversely, expansion might improve student outcomes for various reasons. For example, it would spread the huge
burden of curriculum development across more schools, freeing
staff to spend more time with students. All of these issues compli-
cate the interpretation of Met outcomes.

Absences, Discipline, Mobility, and College Admissions[1]

Attendance is an important measure of student engagement and
interest in schooling. Since the Met emphasizes student interests,
it is proud of its 7% absentee rate, which is one-third the average
20% absentee rate for the other eight Providence high schools. (The
state average is 8%.) Even more striking is the Met's 1.4% rate of
disciplinary suspensions, which is one-*eighteenth* the average 25.4%
suspension rate for other Providence high schools. (The state average is 28.9%.)[2] The Met attributes its low rate of suspensions to two
consequences of being small and personalized: first, that discipline
problems occur less often when students are well known and con-
nected to the community; and second, that the school is committed
to resolving discipline problems without shutting students out of
school.

Dropout and transfer rates are also important indicators of
school effectiveness. Of the 241 students who enrolled in the Met
during its first 4 years, 19 dropped out. This 8% rate is less than
one-third the average 27% dropout rate for the other eight Providence high schools. Most of the 19 students who dropped out had
severe problems related to drugs, crime, health, mental health, and
chaotic homes. They were neglected or abused by their parents,
too depressed to get out of bed, or selling drugs and fighting for
their lives. Most left against the Met's wishes, but a few were asked
to leave after the school's intensive efforts failed to improve the
student's harmful behavior, neglect of schoolwork, or inadequate
attendance.

---

1. Unless otherwise noted, all statistics below are from *Information Works!* (2000), the Rhode
Island Department of Education's yearly compendium.
2. One student may account for multiple suspensions. Therefore, these rates indicate total
suspensions per 100 students, not the total number of students suspended.

"A common theme for many of these students," an advisor
said, "is that even if you helped them find the exact projects they
wanted more than anything in the world, they still couldn't make
themselves buckle down and work. All of my students who
dropped out were really wounded, really hurt inside. It manifested
itself in very different ways for each student, but the bottom line
was that they all did pretty much nothing, no matter what. And
the Met is really only successful with students who can find it
within themselves to try. They get tons of support, but they need
to do part of the work too."

In addition to the 19 dropouts, 26 Met students (11%) transferred to other high schools. (Several more transferred but then
returned.) The state's database does not provide comparable transfer rates for other Providence high schools. Met students transfer
for several reasons. First, because they move. Second, because of
the distance—students who commute from outside Providence are
more than twice as likely to transfer. Third, students transfer for
the same reasons they drop out—family, legal, health, mental
health, and drug problems. Fourth, they crave features of conventional high schools that the Met lacks, such as structured classes
and high-profile sports programs. (In conversations with Met staff,
Ted Sizer has dubbed this condition "school sickness," likening it
to homesickness.) Fifth, some students dislike the Met's intimacy
and crave the anonymity of a large high school. Last, some parents
initiate the transfer because they worry that their child isn't learning
enough, is learning the wrong things, or will lack the credentials
needed for college acceptance.

College admission is the bottom line for many parents, which
is why the Met community relished the front-page headline of the
Providence Journal on June 10, 2000: "First Class Achievement: Every
Graduate of Unusual High School Heading to College." The Met's
46 seniors received a total of 90 acceptance letters from Brown,
Reed, Northeastern, Worcester Polytech, University of Rhode Island, Community College of Rhode Island, and 20 other colleges
from Vermont to Arizona. Most started college right away, five
deferred admission to work or travel, and one entered the Navy.
Collectively they won $400,000 in scholarships. The Met is particu-
larly proud that more than half of these students are the first in
their family ever to attend college.

Test Scores

Today's standardized tests exemplify H. L. Mencken's observation that to every human problem there is an easy solution that is neat, plausible, and wrong. If not obliged by state and college requirements, the Met would not participate in the charade. Among other pitfalls discussed in Chapter 7, these tests yield simple numbers that conceal vital complexities. Dennis illustrated this in a staff memo:

"Presenting our test data is a fascinating puzzle, because it could be done in so many ways. Here are some examples. Our PSAT scores were 10 points below the Rhode Island and national averages. Thus, we are bad. Then you remember that we tested 100% of our students, while the national norms are based on only 52% of all students—usually the college-track ones. That profoundly changes the meaning of our scores. Also, the national PSAT sample is 12% African-American and Latino, compared with 56% at the Met. Even though some students from all racial and ethnic groups score at the highest levels, we know statistically that White students get higher test scores on average. Thus, since we're only 10 points behind, we are good.

"Another example comes from the Rhode Island state exams. Forty-six percent of Providence students met the standards, compared with 18% at the Met. Thus, we are bad. But the citywide figure hides a huge gap. At Classical—the college-prep magnet school—71% met the standards, while all the other city high schools averaged just 13%. Thus, at 18%, we are good. Only by taking a deeper look at the data can we achieve this balanced perspective."

Regardless of whether Met students' scores are seen as high or low, the Met deserves only a portion of the credit or blame. Students take the state exams in spring of 10th grade, after less than 2 years at the Met, and having just spent 8 or more years in mainstream schools. Moreover, Rhode Island's recent adoption of a new state exam makes it difficult to assess progress over time. Most Met students took the old exams in middle school and the new exams in high school, and the two exams can't be compared because they yield different types of scores.

The only test scores that provide data on student progress over time come from the Met's first year. Mostly to enhance public relations, the Met administered the Metropolitan Achievement Test to all students at the beginning and end of ninth grade. Math scores rose by 1.9 grade levels (from 6.5 to 8.4), which increased the students' national percentile ranking by 22 points (from 18% to 40%). Reading scores increased 1.4 grade levels (from 6.8 to 8.2) and nine percentile points (from 29% to 38%). These students were beginning to catch up, gaining more than one grade level in their first year at the Met. Despite the favorable impression conveyed by these scores, the Met saw testing as an unwise use of resources and discontinued it after one year.

Learning Goals

Until appropriate outcome measures have been developed, it will be difficult to quantify student progress toward the Met's learning goals. But that doesn't mean that the learning goals should be abandoned. As Einstein warned us, not everything that counts can be counted, and not everything that can be counted counts. Rather than using quantitative measures, the Met has relied on each student's learning team to assess whether the student made adequate progress each quarter and each year.

Summarizing the progress of 200 students on five learning goals in just a few paragraphs was a perplexing task that felt audacious but seemed important for the purposes of this chapter. The best solution I found was to group the learning goals into three tiers according to students' relative success in achieving them. From most to least successful, the tiers are (1) communication, social reasoning, and personal qualities; (2) empirical reasoning; and (3) quantitative reasoning.

These tiers require two important caveats. First, they are averages, so they blur a wide range of student achievement into a single number. For example, even though the quantitative learning goal falls into the lowest tier, many students have achieved or surpassed it. Second, the tiers compare the Met only to itself, not to other schools. Thus a student who did poorly by Met standards might be considered successful by conventional standards, and vice versa. Moreover, based on the dropout statistics discussed above, many students who failed to excel by Met standards would probably have dropped out of conventional schools.

Relevant to tier three (quantitative reasoning), Dennis says, "Our teachers are outstanding with reading, writing, thinking, social issues, and helping students grow personally, but many of them are less comfortable with math and science. And despite all the progressive mathematicians out there, we haven't been able to hire ones to develop the materials we need to do it right. We've worked hard to figure it out, without a great deal of success. We've gotten our students past the math phobia that most of them arrived here with, and many of them have applied basic math to relatively simple real-world problems. But only a fraction of our students have gained a deep understanding of quantitative reasoning and applied it to complex problems. I would feel really bad if I didn't keep asking myself 'our math compared to what?' Most of the math that our students had in middle school didn't connect to much of anything and didn't stick with them. But it looked good, because it was called Pre-Algebra.

"There is no blame on why we haven't done math well. It's just hard. Connecting math to LTIs is still our long-term goal, but so far we haven't been able to make it work for enough students. Should we continue to encourage LTI math while also establishing a more traditional curriculum that all students have to complete? Our first round of college applications showed us that SAT scores still play a huge role—an absurd role. So we're struggling with whether we should bombard students with concept after concept in hopes of boosting their SAT scores, or whether we should do what we think will be more helpful for the rest of their lives, which is helping them understand a few important concepts in depth. It's tough to admit, but I think we're going to have to make a decision that right now, with the world as it is, we need to do math in some pretty straight ways. That might be the best we can do right now. And at the same time we'll continue developing the alternative approaches that we think make the most sense."

Tier two (empirical reasoning) has been more successful than tier three, but still offers the Met some fundamental challenges. "We've managed to get our students to think scientifically and apply empirical logic to important problems," Dennis says. "But have we reached the level that we're doing empirical reasoning the way we *think* it should be? Not yet. Are our students getting more out of it than they would out of a biology or chemistry class in a conventional school? Absolutely, because most students don't get much out of those classes. They forget it pretty much immediately, and college professors say that most high school students are learning facts that are so oversimplified that basically they're not even true."

"Our students have done some sophisticated real world projects," one advisor says. "What's holding us back is that we haven't developed a sophisticated culture around empirical reasoning, and we're just beginning to develop the support materials that advisors need to do it really well. For example, students often conduct surveys as a way of turning their interests into numbers that they can work with empirically and quantitatively. The problem is that many students aren't fully understanding the data they collect. We need to create a survey module that would lead students through the key aspects—hypothesis generation, sample selection, data collection, analysis, and drawing conclusions. And we need to create those types of materials not just for surveys, but for lots of other types of projects too."

"Most of our teachers lack science backgrounds," the advisor continued, "but that isn't the problem. The problem is that they view empirical reasoning too narrowly. They tend to interpret it as traditional high school science—biology, chemistry, physics, and earth sciences—when in fact the Met's notion of empirical reasoning is much broader than that. The subject matter could be almost anything—from fabric design to social injustice—as long as students are learning logical methods of inquiry and thinking. But most advisors don't seem to think that way yet. We need to continue developing our curriculum to reflect this broader scope. Naturally we still have some hurdles to overcome, but that doesn't mean we should run back to traditional methods that research and experience have shown to be ineffective."

As for tier one—communication, social reasoning, and personal qualities—the Met considers this their greatest success. Many students have made tremendous strides in reading, writing, speaking, listening, and interpreting. They have gained tools to go beyond the popular media when forming opinions. They have improved their persistence, responsibility, cooperation, resourcefulness, and many other personal qualities. They have begun to want to learn, even when no one is looking over their shoulder. And students who were already tier-one standouts when they arrived at the Met have been able to expand their learning experiences far beyond the usual bounds of high school.

Family and Community Involvement

Parents are invited to participate deeply in the Met—not only when problems arise, but from day one; not only to chaperone and bake cookies, but also to help design their child's curriculum and assess their child's progress. At a recent Family Exhibition Night, 40 parents set up displays and discussed their careers and hobbies with students. Ten LTIs eventually resulted from this event. Parents also sit on the school's governing board and committees. They serve as buddies for newer parents, shepherding them through an unfamiliar school experience. Parents are among the invited speakers at graduation, and they sign their child's diploma along with the principal.

Rhode Island's 1999–2000 school survey found stark contrasts between parents at the Met and parents at other Rhode Island schools, as shown in Table 9.1. Despite rhetoric of going "beyond

Table 9.1: Parent Responses on 1999–2000 Rhode Island School Survey

Survey Item	Percentage	
	The Met	*Rhode Island*
Strongly agree:		
I feel welcome at this school	95	49
This school views parents as important partners	98	35
The teachers care about my teen	95	42
This school is one of the best for students and parents	87	27
This school has an active parent organization	87	34
I have spoken with my child's teacher on the phone:		
At least once	95	43
Many times	64	6

the bake sale," few high schools involve parents deeply. But 78% of Met parents (compared with 32% statewide) report that the school does well at including parents on committees such as curriculum, budget, and school improvement. The Met continues to struggle with widely recognized barriers to parent involvement such as transportation and scheduling, but the school has achieved nearly 100% parent participation and offers a model that could inform widespread innovation.

"We've been unusually successful in engaging Latino parents," says Elayne Walker-Cabral, director of family and community relations for The Big Picture Company. "That's because early on we worked closely with a number of Latino families who then became very committed to the school and helped us engage other Latino families. Now they're sending their neighbors and relatives to the school, so we have a stream of families who know about us and want to come here."

As for community involvement, few schools do more. In fact, the centrality of LTIs blurs the boundary between the school and the surrounding community. As Elliot often says, "The *community is the campus.*" In the Met's first 4 years, more than 400 individuals served as LTI mentors. Members of industry and nonprofit groups sit on the Met's governing board, and other community partnerships happen frequently, such as invited guests at daily pick-me-ups and collaborations with local artists. The Met serves the community too, through service learning projects, LTI projects, and hosting frequent visitors who want to study the school's reforms. And once the Met's commons facility is fully built in 2002, it will serve as a community center and commercial space for small community enterprises.

Nontraditional Outcomes

Imagine an efficiency expert assessing productivity at a meditation center: "Why do you stroll on winding paths? Why do you linger over your organic garden? Don't you know that pavement and pesticides would be quicker?" His conventional yardsticks are useless in that setting, and the Met faces a similar dilemma.

Some of the Met's most powerful outcomes are subtle, radical, and hard to measure. Perhaps most central is the school's commitment to fighting for the education of every student. Many high schools try to rid themselves of the most difficult students, as vividly documented by Michelle Fine (1986). She cites, among other insidious practices, the low-friction process in which "six or seven kids a day come into the school's main office asking to be discharged. Nobody says 'Are you kidding? Where do you think you're going?' There is no hysteria, no upset, just a bureaucratic, even pleasant exchange of papers. . . . Most students who leave are not explicitly thrown out. They 'choose' to leave, rarely encouraged to stay" (pp. 400, 405).

Nothing could be less true of the Met. When students want to drop out, the Met mounts a campaign to keep them. The staff address underlying problems, arrange alternatives, emphasize the bleak job prospects for dropouts, try to help parents take a strong stand, enlist the help of internship mentors and fellow students, and even hold sit-ins in students' living rooms. Students are valued as individuals, and they know it. They are not just part of a bureaucratic machine that lacks the structures and resources to deal with them. And the point is not merely to keep students in school, but to help them reach their highest potential. In many schools, low expectations become self-fulfilling prophecies, particularly for disadvantaged students. At the Met, all students are vigorously encouraged toward high achievement, regardless of their background.

The Met also helps low-income students navigate the worlds of higher education and the middle class—foreign worlds that will influence many of their options in life. My father was raised on welfare by his widowed mother in the Cambridge housing projects, but he was a good student and always assumed he would go to college down the street at Harvard. In the spring of senior year, at age 16 and without guidance from a single adult, he filled out and submitted his Harvard application. He was crestfallen when the rejection letter arrived. He had no idea why they didn't want him, and he'd been so confident of being accepted that he hadn't applied anywhere else. During the summer, he applied to Boston University and was accepted. On the first day of classes, he dutifully arrived at 8:00 A.M. and hovered for hours awaiting his homeroom assignment. Finally, to his deep embarrassment, an administrator informed him that universities don't have homerooms. (Five years later he had earned a B.S. and an M.B.A.)

The Met works hard to spare students such indignities. By exposing them to professional work settings and caring mentors, by sending them to conferences and college classes, by teaching them how to identify resources and ask for their due, the Met chips away at the barriers blocking low-income students from opportunities that are routinely available to the middle class. That's how Setya moved from his street gang to the office of a United Way vice-president. That's how Tamika journeyed from the housing projects to the Ivy League.

The Met's success should also be measured by its unwavering commitment to acting on its beliefs and building the diverse constituencies needed to make those actions possible. Many of the Met's innovations have been advocated by prominent national groups such as the Carnegie Foundation, the National Association of Secondary School Principals, and the U.S. Department of Education, but the Met is one of at most a handful of American schools that have managed to put these innovations into practice with such intensity and fidelity.

By its very existence, the Met could alter the terms of the school reform debate. In the long run, that could be its strongest influence. Just as the Coalition of Essential Schools has catalyzed reforms beyond its 1,000 member schools, The Big Picture Company hopes to leverage the Met's initial success into a burgeoning of small schools, personalized learning, internships, exhibitions, learning teams, senior projects, and other aspects of their model. Within Rhode Island and beyond, the Met's example has already eased the way for reforms in many schools. And, as detailed in the next chapter, many educators around the country have worked with The Big Picture Company to incorporate features of the Met into new or existing schools.

Conclusion

By conventional standards, the Met's 100% college-acceptance rate is the clearest evidence that something is working. There is little doubt that many Met students who are now college-bound would have dropped out of mainstream high schools or ended their formal education at age 18—many students say so themselves. And even if they had graduated from a mainstream high school, it's difficult to imagine that Tamika, Cesar, and many others would have flourished so remarkably.

But the Met is not for everyone, nor does it succeed with all students. Traditionalists who expect all students to master a standardized classical curriculum will never be satisfied with the Met. Nor will those at the other end of the spectrum, who believe that all student learning should be self-directed.

Then there are the students who would succeed at any high school. Does the Met offer them enough advantages to offset the risk of attending a school whose approach is not fully tested? Conversely, for students who will succeed anywhere, why risk attending mainstream schools that *have* been fully tested and found to have significant shortcomings? These judgments rely on deeply held individual values, which is why ultimately the only workable solution may be to provide multiple public schooling models and allow parents to choose for their own children.

Four teachers and high-level administrators at the Met and The Big Picture Company have a child of high school age. It's notable that three out of the four, including Elliot Washor, send their children to the Met. This is a rarity among inner-city schools, and a compelling testament to the Met's value. These parents are middle class and college educated, and their children could have attended the college-prep magnet school in Providence or the state's top-ranked public high school in a nearby suburb.

Clearly, the Met has its problems. LTIs fall through, students drop out, personalities clash, learning goals need clarification, and more. Fully transforming the Met's principles into practice will require years of energetic development. But utopia is not one of the alternatives. Innovative schools are often compared to some nonexistent ideal, rather than to existing models that have well-documented flaws. People who demand guarantees before allowing schools to embark on promising reforms are either naïve or just trying to get in the way. There is ample evidence that the Met works well for students of many backgrounds and outperforms many high schools that serve similar students. The Met's approach deserves a long-term trial and increased attention from educators, parents, researchers, and policymakers.

10 Surviving and Expanding

There is no shortage of stories about schools that have beaten the odds. An article in the local paper applauds the teacher or principal whose tireless work and cutting-edge strategies have reversed a downward spiral. Other schools soon climb aboard, eager to use the winning strategies with their own students. But all too often the newcomers fall short, and even the original school backslides into mediocrity.

The Met's founders are determined to avoid that pattern. From the outset they designed the Met to be a demonstration school, a laboratory for developing educational innovations that could be adopted by others. This chapter discusses the tremendous challenges they will face in pursuing that mission. To help explain where they're headed, the next section offers a brief history of where they've been. More Met history can be found in Sarason (1998, pp. 88–95) and Walker and MacDonald (1996).

Lightning Strikes Once

Without a remarkable convergence of talents and opportunities, the Met never would have left the drawing boards. Dennis and Elliot were working in New Hampshire until 1993, but they had two powerful allies in Rhode Island. Ted Sizer was the director of the Annenberg Institute for School Reform at Brown University, managing the largest philanthropic donation ($500 million) in the history of public education. Ten years earlier Sizer had launched the Coalition of Essential Schools, with Dennis as one of his first and most successful principals. The second ally was Stanley Goldstein, CEO of a group of companies that included CVS Pharmacy,

Rhode Island's largest for-profit employer. While Dennis and Elliot were still in New Hampshire, Goldstein funded a project of theirs that later won the prestigious Innovations in State and Local Government award from the Ford Foundation and Harvard University.

Sizer brought Dennis and Elliot to Annenberg in 1994, and they soon launched an initiative to move Rhode Island toward interest-based and experiential models of education. (This initiative later became The Big Picture Company.) Three catalysts were already in place: A community coalition had released a high-profile report calling for comprehensive education reform (Public Education Fund, 1993); Rhode Island had recently hired Peter McWalters, a reform-minded commissioner of education; and a state bond issue had just been passed to build a new regional career and technical high school. The school's initial design had already been created by consultant Charles Mojkowski, and it proposed a stronger integration of academic and vocational education than was typical in Rhode Island or nationwide.

Dennis and Elliot developed alliances with McWalters, Mojkowski, and many other key people in Rhode Island's educational and political circles. In the summer of 1995, they successfully lobbied for oversight of the new school. After a frenzied year of planning, building coalitions, managing public relations, and recruiting students and staff, the Metropolitan Regional Career and Technical Center opened in September of 1996.

"Creating a public institution as innovative as the Met requires support from a huge number of people," Elliot says. "Dennis and I had just arrived from rural New Hampshire into a tightly knit, multiracial city like Providence. Our ambitious proposals couldn't have gotten very far without a great many people at all levels who put their personal and professional reputations on the line in support of what we were trying to accomplish. Governor Almond and his staff really helped us out, and we had great support from Paul Crowley, Charlie Walton, and others in the General Assembly who helped us convince some of their more skeptical colleagues. The same is true for Fred Lippitt and Mary Harrison on the Board of Regents. Commissioner McWalters was particularly instrumental in persuading the General Assembly and the Board of Regents of the value of our programmatic, fiscal, and physical designs, all of which were very unconventional. He continued to support us right through the Met's first 4 years and the success of our first graduating class.

"And we never could have succeeded without Stanley Goldstein, who by that time had agreed to be the chairman of our board. He's been in Rhode Island all his life, everyone knows him, and CVS is one of the state's largest employers. Dennis had a great national reputation as a principal, but Stanley's local reputation helped us gain the political clout we needed. We also hired Elayne Walker and Keith Oliveira, who had grown up in Providence and had worked extensively with local community development organizations. They both had strong ties to the Latino and African-American communities here, and their support was essential to building the broad community coalition we needed to run a successful school.

"It's amazing that so many pieces were already in place. Stanley, Peter, Ted, Annenberg, and the Coalition of Essential Schools were all in Rhode Island, the bond issue was already passed, and Charlie Mojkowski's design proposal was within striking distance of our vision. Everything was a huge struggle, but without those pieces in place it would have been even harder."

Scale-Up Challenges

Waiting for lightning to strike twice is not a winning strategy. In an ideal world, the most effective social programs would be widely replicated, because well-informed "consumers" would select the best "products." But in the real world, powerful vested interests can sustain ineffective programs and marginalize exemplary ones. Innovative schools, even highly successful ones, face tremendous obstacles to scaling up.

"We're not trying to create a bunch of copycat schools that look exactly like the Met," Dennis says. "Our goal is to bring our learning *principles* to other settings. But the bottom line is that our model is going to be very difficult to replicate. It's a huge change from the mainstream system. The only way it will really take hold is if many more people begin to realize that the system needs a major overhaul. Right now very few people really believe that. If the world changes in the ways that many pundits are predicting, then our model will become popular. But if the world keeps pushing for more standardization and small thinking, then we'll always be on the fringes."

Many changes would have to take place for Big Picture schools to proliferate. "The Met's approach to learning would be impossible without our freedom from certain state mandates," Dennis says. "Seat-time requirements would make LTIs impossible, and required course sequences would do away with personalized projects. Union contracts are another huge issue. Our teachers met with both unions and decided against joining. But if they *had* unionized, we couldn't have existed in our current form without special contract provisions for scheduling and hiring. Most contracts would prohibit our 20 days per year of planning and staff-development time, even though we pay our teachers for the extra days. We also have after-school meetings and ask teachers to be available one night per week for different events. That cuts into teachers' usual time off, but how can we do family involvement if we're only available from 8 A.M. to 3 P.M. on weekdays? Under many union contracts, we wouldn't even be able to choose our own teachers! Just imagine a corporation that couldn't hire or fire its own executives—it's mind-boggling.

"The bottom line is local control. We need the freedom to be able to hire teachers who fit our needs. We need assurance that our principal won't be transferred to another school at the whim of a district administrator. Local schools should be given more power, and substantial debate and justification should be required for anything that the *district* wants to control—not the other way around."

When burdened by too many external constraints, innovative schools fall short of their potential. They are unable to implement their model as they intended, so it never receives a genuine trial. And as the number of innovative schools grows, so do the obstacles. Lisbeth Schorr (1997) cites a study of 10 award-winning New York City principals who all admitted that their success relied on quietly sidestepping the system's rules. A few schools can play that game, but as their numbers grow they attract more attention and the loopholes close. Then further innovation can happen only by changing the system, which is one of The Big Picture Company's primary goals.

One of the Met's strongest efforts at changing systems has been with college admissions officers. These gatekeepers typically rank applicants based on numbers that the Met can't provide (e.g., grades, credits, and class rank) or that measure Met learning poorly (e.g., SAT scores). The Met believes that student portfolios and teacher narratives are better indicators of a student's achievement and potential, but many colleges are unwilling or unable to devote the extra time needed to review and rank those more complex materials.

The Met hired a veteran college counselor and met with dozens of colleges to explain the school's approach to learning. The school persuaded several colleges to interview every Met student who applied, knowing that many students would be more impressive in person than on paper. With every application, the Met sent a detailed description of the school and a one-page transcript that admissions officers could read quickly if they lacked the time to review the lengthier materials that most students also submitted.

The first half of the transcript includes test scores, college courses taken, and highlights of the student's projects. The second half is an elaborate grid listing the Met's learning goals and the main strategies by which the student achieved them. For each learning goal, the student receives one of the following ratings: (1) exceeded expectations with distinction; (2) exceeded expectations; (3) achieved expectations; or (4) still in progress. Met advisors were very reluctant to assign these pseudo-grades, but they knew that many colleges disqualify applications that lack grades or grade equivalents.

The fact that every Met graduate was accepted to college suggests that these efforts met some measure of success, but many obstacles remain. Some colleges had strict SAT cutoffs, and others required specific course distributions (e.g., four years of English classes) even if applicants could provide strong evidence that they had achieved comparable learning in other ways. Admissions directors have told Dennis that they value students from innovative schools but have not yet updated the policies that block those students from being admitted. The Met hopes to reduce these obstacles and aid scale-up efforts by actively promoting its students and its model.

Successful scale-up will also require new accountability systems, because most state exams are poor measures of Met learning. The Met believes in its consensus-based system of assessment but expects to encounter resistance during scale-up from those who want a more standardized approach. That dilemma might be resolved by the alternative accountability systems that some districts have already started to develop. A group of small schools in New York City hopes to create review committees composed of parents, teachers, college professors, community members, and sister schools. The system would also include "panels composed of critical friends and more distanced and skeptical publics, demanding convincing evidence that the school was on the right track and acting responsibly" (Schorr, 1997, p. 127).

Another fundamental scale-up issue is how fast each school should change. Many reformers argue that moving too fast is politically infeasible, but Ted Sizer counters that "a little change is no change at all. Gradual reform might be easier in the short run, but it serves the ultimate goal badly. Everything important in a school affects everything else, and if synergy among the key elements is not achieved, the result is frustration. Essential schools that take the gradual approach appear to be having a harder time of reform than those that are able to charge ahead with a comprehensive plan" (1996, p. 100).

It's not difficult to imagine problems that would result from piecemeal adoption of Big Picture reforms. Students can't immerse themselves in their interests and also carry a traditional course load. Teachers can't supervise in-depth, personalized projects and also teach five classes per day.

On the other hand, scaling up too quickly has its own perils. The Met's initial plan was to open six small schools in 4 years, but, due to construction delays, it was possible to open only two. (The other four are scheduled to open in September 2002.) "It's been a godsend that they haven't opened as fast as we initially wanted," Dennis says. "Knowing how hard we've worked just to get two schools going, the thought of having been much bigger is terrifying. So we're going at just the right speed."

In addition to the huge task of starting a school, the Met was also creating its curriculum from scratch, designing its buildings, fighting for credibility, and disseminating its work broadly. If the model scaled up to more schools, that burden would become lighter per school. An effective middle ground might be for new schools to start out very small but implement the entire model from day one. In large school buildings, that could happen by adopting a school-within-a-school design as discussed in Chapter 2.

But most school districts want gradual change, despite the probable pitfalls. "In the past I haven't really wanted to talk to schools that are trying to make small changes," Dennis said recently. "I don't know if anything really changes at deeper levels when they approach it that way. But now sometimes I'll say, 'If you can't make huge changes, why don't you try out a *couple* of these concepts?' My top priority is for students to be doing real work with an adult who shares their interests. Maybe Big Picture should be helping schools figure out how to do that within their own constraints. One good niche would be 12th-grade programs around the country, because no one knows what to do with seniors. And then maybe it would trickle down to lower grades."

Then there's the money question. Does the Met cost more than other schools? Does it cost less? The Met's per-pupil allotment from public funds is about equal to the average of other Providence high schools, but several other factors should also be considered. First, the Met's start-up years will probably cost more than later years. Second, what dollar figure should be assigned to the resources provided by LTI sites? Do those resources increase the Met's bottom line, or do students provide enough value in return to call it an even trade? Third, all public schools have grant income and subtle costs or benefits that don't show up in official budgets. For example, the Met's high graduation rate is likely to cause a marked reduction in their students' lifetime use of public welfare resources (Carnegie Council on Adolescent Development, 1989). Failing to include those savings on the Met's balance sheet would reflect the fiscal shortsightedness that sabotages much of our public spending. Until sophisticated econometric analyses such as these are carried out, it will be difficult to provide a meaningful answer to the cost question.

"We could run the Met with whatever money we got," Dennis says. "If we had half as much money, there would be things you wouldn't see, but we'd still be doing the same basic model. We'll always ask for about the same funding that other schools get, and then we bring in little grants whenever we can. Right now we get a little extra money because we're in the same funding stream as vocational schools, but there will be other times when funding gets tighter and it will all be leveled out. And during the development phase of a new school you really need some extra money. That was especially true for getting LTIs going, which would have been very hard without the 3 years of support we received from the Human Resource Investment Council to hire Elaine Hackney to develop our workplace connections. She made contacts with hospitals and businesses, created orientation and project design materials, made a database of contacts, developed evaluation forms, arranged events to honor mentors, and more."

Perhaps the paramount obstacle to scale-up is American willingness to tolerate widespread school inequities and failures. In his article "Only for *My* Kid: How Privileged Parents Undermine School Reform," Alfie Kohn (1998a) argues that many parents fight to preserve the inequities that benefit their own child. These parents, predominantly White and middle class, are often the most outspoken members of their communities. They want the grading systems that elevate their own child's status and the "gifted and talented" programs in which their own child reaps a disproportionate share of school resources. Rather than the naked racism of earlier generations, these parents justify their actions by citing the apathy and misbehavior of "lower-track" students. But that apathy and misbehavior may be fueled in part by the special status and extra resources bestowed on "higher-track" students.

Kohn (1998a) cites research in which parents have vigorously objected to improving conditions for other children, even if no resources would be taken away from their own child. He argues that, for many parents, the point of schooling "is not to get an education but to get ahead," so they oppose reforms that threaten their already sizable slice of the pie (p. 573). Kohn also cites research in which parents declared their support for more equitable models of education until they discovered that putting those ideals into practice would interfere with the advantages they were seeking for their own child. These findings reconfirm the obvious chasm that separates America's egalitarian rhetoric from its social-Darwinist reality.

Our willingness to tolerate inequities also extends to entire schools and districts. Affluent families enroll their children in private schools or well-funded suburban districts, but many other schools and districts have few resources and dismal outcomes. This crisis is obscured by the intensive but inadequate remediation efforts of many low-performing districts. Chicago recently placed the lowest performing fifth of its schools on probation and pledged to shut them down if they fail to improve after receiving intensive help from the city. Ron Wolk (1998) spotlights the criterion by which these schools were placed on probation, namely that 85% or more of their students were reading below grade level. Clearly those schools need intensive help, but why the 85% cutoff? If 50% or 30% of students are reading below grade level, shouldn't that be enough to call in the cavalry?

Only if the school district has enough horses. The problem is that lowering the cutoff even to 50% would have landed *three out of every four* Chicago schools on probation. Instead the city chose a cutoff that acknowledged a tremendous problem—one-fifth of all schools on probation—but also fostered the illusion that the remaining schools *weren't* failing. Such illusions save Chicago (and many other school districts) from an act that institutions abhor—pointing the finger at themselves. Wolk (1998) argues that since nearly all Chicago schools are failing, surely the fault lies within the larger system, which hasn't provided them with what they need to succeed.

These problems go beyond just the educational system. Schools are only one of many institutions whose structures undermine our society's professed goals of justice and democracy. Michelle Fine (1986) argues that "school-based reforms need to be developed in tandem with a package of economic and social reforms, including job programs, provision of child care, funded access to contraception and abortion services, balanced housing development, social and health services, and so forth, and ultimately there needs to be a redistribution of resources and power within society. Targeting schools as the only site for social change and hope for the next generation deflects attention and resources, critique and anger away from insidious economic and social inequities" (p. 407). In short, the efforts of the Met and The Big Picture Company are just one of many crucial levels at which the fight for social justice must proceed.

Building Capacity for Scale-Up

Imagine that a large number of districts decided to launch Big Picture schools, that parents and community members supported the decision, and that governments, unions, and colleges made the necessary accommodations. Several significant obstacles would still remain. First, who would staff the schools? Conventional teacher training is poorly suited to the Big Picture model (and to conventional models, for that matter), and many states and colleges are struggling to improve their training programs.

Consider my own current quest for teacher certification at a college in Rhode Island. The college insists that for math certification I need additional courses in algebra and geometry, even though I've taken 4 years of calculus and have an electrical engineering degree from MIT. Nor do I meet the course requirements for English certification, despite my undergraduate English minor and having published this book and other writings. None of the four required courses in British literature can be swapped for African, Asian, Latin, or Native American literature, even though those groups comprise 78% of Providence students and 37% nationwide (National Center for Education Statistics, 1999; Rhode Island Department of Education, 2000a). Finally, my 3 years of teaching college undergraduates wouldn't reduce the required amount of student teaching.

The college also requires six courses about the theory and practice of education. My first skirmish was seeking exemption from the introductory psychology class, which I foolishly assumed would be automatic because of my Ph.D. in psychology and years as a researcher and therapist.

"Do you know the XYZ theory of adolescent development?" the department chair asked.

"Never heard of it," I replied.

"How about the PDQ theory?"

"Nope."

"Well, you *have* taken quite a few psychology courses."

"Yes, 30 of them."

"Hmmm . . . " he said, reshuffling my transcripts, as if perhaps he'd missed something incriminating the first time through. Then he quizzed me on my therapist credentials and research findings, making full use of his training as a chemist. Finally he glowered at me, cleared his throat, and signed the exemption form.

With that settled, there were still five education courses that I did have to take. They were the most undemanding and unsubstantive courses I have ever taken. The special education text was 30 years old, and the instructor missed the first class because he didn't realize we were starting that week. Another instructor squelched anyone who disagreed with him. One course had no assigned readings whatsoever, and two other courses assigned fewer than 50 pages for the entire semester. None of our meager assignments required library or Internet research, and across all five courses I had to develop only two lessons for use in actual classrooms. To prepare us for the rigors of classroom life in the new millennium, one professor even lectured and tested us on educational priorities in ancient Egypt.

Despite training that is often inadequate, many teachers enter the classroom with passion, creativity, and dedication. The Met looks for these qualities and has assembled a talented staff, but extensive scale-up would require new training programs. Ideally, state regulations would also be changed to permit the certification of candidates with appropriate skills but unconventional backgrounds.

In reference to a high school that shares many features with the Met, Willis Hawley (1991) writes that such schools "place huge demands on teachers—emotional commitments to students and peers, the ability to teach across subjects, the capacity to learn new things and adapt accordingly, and to learn from each other. It is not clear that we can find enough teachers with these values and strengths unless the benefits of being a teacher are substantially increased. These benefits include salaries and working conditions which will attract and retain people who now pursue other professions, and the status that society accords to persons whose work we believe is both complex and essential to maintaining our quality of life" (p. xi).

Many of these teacher training issues also apply to principals, which motivated The Big Picture Company to create the Principal Residency Network, a training program for principals of innovative, personalized schools. Their training model has much in common with the Met's approach to education. A mentor principal provides intensive mentorship to an aspiring principal who already works in the same school. Together they design a personalized learning plan that gives the aspiring principal increasing responsibility for administrative tasks such as preparing budgets and managing crises. These projects have real-life consequences that motivate aspiring principals to meet high standards. Aspiring principals give exhibitions twice per year to demonstrate their progress, and on completing the program they receive a principal certification from one of three partner universities.

Three Met staff members—Amy Bayer, Jill Homberg, and Charlie Plant—have completed this training program. Starting with the 2000–2001 school year, they became the front-line directors of the Met's two small schools. Dennis and Elliot still provide supervision but have stepped back from day-to-day principal duties. Now they spend more time on other Big Picture projects, including the creation of the Met's other four small schools. Future graduates of the Principal Residency Network will become the directors of those four schools. And with a $1.3 million grant from the DeWitt Wallace–Reader's Digest Fund, The Big Picture Company has created three new network sites in New England and is laying groundwork for national scale-up. They expect to certify 200 new school leaders by 2005. Details of the Principal Residency Network can be found in a series of chapters authored by its students and staff (Littky, Allen, & Barth, in press) and in a chapter of Roland Barth's latest book about the principalship (2001).

It is often said that ground-breaking social programs like the Met can succeed only with charismatic leaders like Dennis and Elliot at the helm. But from studies of programs that scaled up successfully, Schorr (1997) concludes that this belief "is not borne out by the evidence. It is true that miracle workers are often the only ones who can overcome the most formidable systems obstacles, especially in jurisdictions and domains where it's never been done before. But as experience with slaying the systems dragon accumulates, those skills can be taught too. Many successful initiatives have found that when their mission is inspiring, they are able to attract people with the courage, ingenuity, and skills the jobs call for" (p. 9).

Schorr (1997) also notes that "leaders of prize-winning public programs have many skills in common that are not mysterious and can be learned." The Principal Residency Network explicitly teaches many of these skills, which include "the willingness to experiment and take risks; to manage by 'groping along'; to tolerate ambiguity; to win the trust of line workers, politicians, and the public; to respond to demands for prompt, tangible evidence of results; to be collaborative in working with staff; and to allow staff discretion at the front lines" (p. 9).

Another scale-up challenge would be finding LTIs for growing numbers of students. Rhode Island has 13 working adults for every high school student, but the number of willing and appropriate mentors is still unknown. As demand for mentors increased, would finding one become harder (because the supply was drying up) or easier (because mentoring became more mainstream and systematized)? Would mentors' commitment grow or diminish over time? Would management applaud or begrudge the time their employees devoted to mentoring? Would participating organizations earn tax breaks as they would for charitable donations? How would mentoring happen in rural areas where potential LTI sites were sprawled across long distances?

Many schools and districts—mostly low-income urban ones—have already contacted The Big Picture Company for help with reform. But Dennis and Elliot believe that their model could also be integrated successfully into middle-class suburban schools whose students are seeking admission to the most competitive universities. They believe that colleges would be impressed with the complexity and sophistication of students' projects, and that students would also have earned high scores on Advanced Placement exams in one or two subject areas that they had pursued in depth. The Coalition of Essential Schools, another Progressive reform model, has been replicated effectively in middle-class districts (Sizer, 1996), and Big Picture hopes to do the same.

The Big Picture Company also anticipates supporting the development of other schools that adopt Big Picture principles. An effective intermediary organization appears to be essential for successful scale-up (Schorr, 1997), and Big Picture is already serving that role for the Met and a K–8 charter school in Providence. They are also preparing to support the 12 new Big Picture schools whose creation is being supported by the Gates Foundation.

Conclusion

In the world of systemic school reform, Yale professor emeritus Seymour Sarason is the voice of unrelenting realism. His dozens of books include such portentous titles as *Psychology Misdirected* and *The Predictable Failure of School Reform*. After reviewing a draft of this book, he urged me to emphasize the myriad factors that make it extremely difficult to create an innovative school either from the ground up or by transforming an existing school. He also warned that detractors would write off the Met by charging that it has succeeded only by lowering standards for student achievement. That charge, he insisted, would be "an egregious falsehood and unfairness."

Sarason wrote a chapter about the Met in his 1998 book on charter schools. (The Met is much like a charter school but technically isn't one.) "This truly innovative school is unlike any other new school I have observed," Sarason concluded, " . . . because the creators were crystal clear about what they wanted to achieve, what the important problems would be, the different ways they could overcome them or dilute their force, the crucial significance of developing diverse kinds of supportive networks and constituencies, the bedrock importance of sincerely involving parents, and that vigilance about values and goals has to be constant and never-ending because it is the price paid for the opportunity to remain free from stifling tradition" (p. 94).

That set of success factors is a fitting blueprint for The Big Picture Company's scale-up efforts. They know that successful Progressive schools have been resented and resisted far more often than they have been imitated. Many onlookers have found the Met exemplary and compelling, but, as noted in an early Big Picture document, "exemplars by themselves do not compel anything" (Walker & McDonald, 1996, p. 14). So rather than idly awaiting a flock of devotees, Big Picture has been publicizing the Met's successes and supporting it's development, building the capacity to support a larger network of schools, and developing partnerships with like-minded individuals and organizations nationwide. The Gates Foundation grant has spurred the initial planning for 12 more Big Picture schools in the next 5 years, but it will be many more years before we know the full extent and impact of the Met and its descendants.

11 Leaving the Nest

Dear Emily,

Four years ago my son was about to drop out of school. He felt like a failure, and he had closed his mind to learning. I heard about the Met and was hopeful. Since then he has evolved into a wonderful, well-rounded individual. The going was rough at times, but you always hung in there. You found ways to help him learn, think, and succeed. Now he seeks out knowledge and has high expectations for himself. Without you and the Met, he would have been one of those statistics where everyone wonders what went wrong. I will forever be grateful to you and the other gifted teachers and staff who worked long hours to provide such a rich, nurturing, safe, and engaging environment for my son. In appreciation and love,

Lisa Foster (Robert's mom)

Dear Doc,

It's been 2 months since graduation, and I'm gradually processing what happened to me these past 4 years. The Met opened my eyes really wide, and it's been more than just surpassing the stereotypes of the inner city. I've developed so much passion and determination to keep on learning, to explore the world and make change in it. There's something in me now that keeps me excited and my mind going all the time. I feel so empowered and free, because I realize that I can do anything if I try hard enough. Sometimes I just feel overwhelmed with emotion.

A couple of weeks ago, my friend and I were having a heavy talk about our schools. We were filled with so much inspiration and love for our schools that we just ran outside and screamed at the top of our lungs "I love life!" It was an amazing moment for me, Doc. The Met will always be in me. It will guide me when I'm in college, and after that maybe I'll start my own Met somewhere. Who knows? Anything is possible. I couldn't have come this far without the support of everyone at the Met. Thank you for everything you've done. I owe you, Doc. I love you.

Tamika

Like everything at the Met, departure happens one student at a time. In addition to proms and beach trips, the school holds a separate farewell event for each graduate. Known as final exhibitions, these events have four parts: the senior project overview, the valedictory address, the advisor address, and the diploma signing.

At most schools, the student who earns top class rank is named valedictorian and delivers an address at graduation. But rather than elevating one student above all others, the Met prefers to honor all graduates for what they have achieved. Consistent with the Latin *valedicere*, which means "to say farewell," every Met graduate delivers a valedictory address during the final week of school. Standing at a podium before 20 or 30 students, staff, parents, and invited guests, each graduate reflects publicly on her growth, her plans, and the people who have nurtured her development.

Following the valedictory address, the advisor offers an extended reflection on the student's years at the Met: "When Solana arrived here in ninth grade, she was already bright, responsible, confident, caring, and hilariously funny. She's leaving with all those same strengths, but the difference is that now she's fully aware of them. Solana and I always used to argue about careers and colleges, because my sights were set much higher than hers. But now she has high expectations too, and her transformation has been beautiful.

"Solana has done superb projects on physical therapy, AIDS, poetry, environmentalism, and many other topics—and senior year has been more of the same. The Girls' Math Group was her official senior project, but she also did college coursework, an LTI at children's hospital, tireless work on the yearbook, and editing her autobiography over and over until it was really polished. She worked hard at college applications and was accepted to Temple, Northeastern, Rhode Island College, and others. She'll be the first person in her family to graduate from high school or attend college, and I'm confident that she will be very successful.

"Even though Solana has been a stellar student, my favorite part has been our personal relationship. She helped everyone in our advisory, myself included, to gain the wonderful personal qualities that she already has in such abundance. She kicked me out of advisory when she knew I needed to eat. She brought flowers and food to my house when I was sick. She even taught me Spanish. But what I will miss most about Solana is that she's my friend, my sister, my student, and sometimes my daughter—*mi hija*. Solana, you were always there for *me* if I had a tough day, not just the other way around. I want to thank you for everything, and for being someone I can be so proud of. I will miss sharing my days with you."

The details varied from student to student, but all advisors spoke with a beaming pride and a sense of shared journeying that could only be described as parental. Few public schools provide the opportunity for all students to be so well known and so deeply loved by their teachers. And judging from students' valedictory addresses, the feeling is mutual. Some were shy and some were effusive, but one student after another crafted an address that flowed from the heart as well as the head. In keeping with Cesar's passion for poetry, he concluded his valediction with these verses:

> I came into this willing, chilling,
> With plans for my future
> That had to do with killing.
> But I changed,
> My thoughts rearranged.
> I don't want to kill,
> But I don't want to be plain.
> I'm willing to change.

I knew I had something,
So I stopped fronting
And opened my mind.
That's when I realized
That everyone looked up to me—
My little sisters, my brothers,
And the rest of my family.

So what was I to do?
I couldn't turn back then.
I had to set an example,
And I've been trying ever since.
I'm going to make something of myself,
Live well, make money,
And share most of my wealth.

And to think that at one point
I was willing to take *your* life.
But this school stuck with me
And helped me re-track my sights.
Where would I have been without the Met?
What would I be doing right now?
Probably making money,
Taking care of a kid,
Still doing what I did—
Maybe even some lethal bids.

But being here I found out
That I expected more of myself,
And I give all credit
To the streets and to the Met,
And especially to my advisor Hal,
The man who guided me
Through the highway of life.
I love you, man.
You taught me not to be afraid,
And how to be a powerful leader,
And I hope I made you proud
When I ran town meetings.

But now we're all on our way,
So as we move ahead
And claim a college set,
We will never forget
We come from the Met.

Later that week, an ivy-covered hall at Brown University pulsed with last-minute preparations for the Met's first graduation ceremony. Cesar seated his family and then merged with his classmates into a sea of royal blue gowns. The hall resounded from the hundreds of dreamers whose years of collective struggle had converged upon this one precious moment. Then the first notes of "Pomp and Circumstance" filled the air, carrying the graduates forward on a torrent of joyful tears and a standing ovation that reached for the future.

Afterword

As co-founders of the Met, we were overjoyed by the Met's first graduation ceremony. We knew that the school, and the vision for school change it represents, had reached a milestone—a moment of truth. It really *is* possible to educate kids differently, starting with their interests. It really *is* possible that colleges and universities—including some of the most selective schools in the country—can see the achievement and promise of our kids and accept them for admission, despite a transcript that looks nothing like that of a traditional high school student. It *is* the case that passionate teachers, personalized learning, and frequent intersections between school and the real world can awake in kids a self-confidence and a passion for learning they didn't know they had.

But as remarkable as that first graduation was, what happened next was even more remarkable: Our kids kept succeeding. National statistics suggest that at least half of this group of college freshmen, most of them from minority groups and the first in their family to seek higher education, would fail. But they are not failing. Now beginning their sophomore year, very few have dropped out or taken a leave. And they have been joined by the next wave of Met graduates, whose college acceptances were every bit as impressive as the class before them.

Are we saying that the Met is the answer to all that ails American education? No. But we believe the Met embodies many of the answers: small personalized schools, adults who know students well, and academics learned through student interests and real-world problem solving.

It seems ironic that in a nation founded in celebration of individualism, we still insist on educating our kids as if they all think the same way, learn the same way, and are motivated in the same way. Most of us were schooled that way, so we accept it as inevitable. The notion of educating "one kid at a time" seems impossible, utopian. But, as Eliot Levine illuminates so clearly, our Met community has found a way.

One Kid at a Time tells the stories of many students whose lives have been changed by the opportunities they found at the Met. We are thrilled to have made a difference for them, but our larger concern is for the countless students whose education falls short of its potential. With the help of the Bill and Melinda Gates Foundation, we are beginning to create other schools that share the Met's approach. But the dominant forces in education continue to sing from a sheet of music that is both out of date and out of tune: more tests, more standardization, and large, impersonal schools.

The fact is that those approaches don't work, and all of us with a stake in America's children can't afford to keep singing the same old song. Across the country, we have met countless people who share our vision and who are working toward a better education for our children. All kinds of people: parents, teachers, principals, policymakers, employers, and many others. We hope that this book will support their attempts to embrace that vision.

If this book strikes a chord with you, we hope that you will take the next step. Visit our website at www.bigpicture.org. Or work for change in your school or your community. Real school change is bigger than just changing schools. It's about changing all kinds of patterns of thinking and doing, inside and outside of schools.

It will take many people to do this work, and we have just begun. As we like to say at the Met: "Here we go!"

Dennis Littky
Elliot Washor
May 2001

References

Barker, R. G., & Gump, P. V. (1964). *Big school, small school: High school size and student behavior.* Stanford, CA: Stanford University Press.

Barth, R. S. (2001). On becoming a principal. In *Learning by heart* (pp. 119–141). San Francisco: Jossey-Bass.

Bombardieri, M. (1999, December 16). Educators' response at issue in Peabody. *The Boston Globe,* pp. A1, B12.

Carnegie Council on Adolescent Development. (1989). *Turning points: Preparing American youth for the 21st century.* New York: Carnegie Corporation.

Cotton, K. (1996). *School size, school climate, and student performance* (School Improvement Research Series, Close-Up #20). Portland, OR: Northwest Regional Educational Laboratory.

Cremin, L. A. (1976). *Public education.* New York: Basic Books.

Cushman, K. (1994). Less is more: The secret of being essential. *Horace, 11*(2), 1–12.

Cushman, K. (1997). Why small schools are essential. *Horace, 13*(3), 1–8.

Dewey, J. (1963). *Experience and education.* New York: Collier Books. (Original work published 1938)

Dewey, J. (1984). *John Dewey: The later works, 1925–1953, Vol. 2: 1925–1927.* Carbondale, IL: Southern Illinois University Press. (Original work published 1926)

Fine, M. (1986). Why urban adolescents drop into and out of high school. *Teachers College Record, 87*(3), 393–409.

Gardner, H. (1991). *The unschooled mind: How children think and how schools should teach.* New York: Basic Books.

Gardner, H. (1999). *The disciplined mind: What all students should understand.* New York: Simon and Schuster.

Goleman, D. (1995). *Emotional intelligence.* New York: Bantam.

Goleman, D. (1998). *Working with emotional intelligence.* New York: Bantam.

Haller, E. J., Monk, D. H., Spotted Bear, A., Griffith, J., & Moss, P. (1990). School size and comprehensiveness: Evidence from high school and beyond. *Educational Evaluation and Policy Analysis, 12*(2), 109–120.

Hawley, W. D. (1991). Public policy and public commitments to enable school restructuring. In E. J. Trickett, *Living an idea: Empowerment and the evolution of an alternative high school* (pp. 5–11). Cambridge, MA: Brookline Books.

Herrera, L., Sipe, C. L., & McClanahan, W. S. (2000). *Mentoring school-age children: Relationship development in community-based and school-based programs.* New York: Public/Private Ventures.

Kammeraad-Campbell, S. (1989). *Doc: Dennis Littky's fight for a better school.* New York: Contemporary Books.

Kemple, J. J., Poglinco, S. M., & Snipes, J. C. (1999). *Career academies: Building career awareness and work-based learning activities through employer partnerships.* New York: Manpower Demonstration Research Corporation.

Klonsky, M. (1995). *Small schools: The numbers tell a story.* Chicago: Small Schools Workshop, University of Illinois at Chicago.

Kohl, H. R. (1998). *The discipline of hope: Learning from a lifetime of teaching.* New York: Simon and Schuster.

Kohn, A. (1998a). Only for *my* kid: How privileged parents undermine school reform. *Phi Delta Kappan, 79*(8), 568–577.

Kohn, A. (1998b). *What to look for in a classroom . . . and other essays.* San Francisco: Jossey-Bass.

Kohn, A. (1999). *The schools our children deserve: Moving beyond traditional classrooms and "tougher" standards.* Boston: Houghton Mifflin.

Lee, V. E., & Smith, J. B. (1994). *Effects of high school restructuring and size on gains in achievement and engagement for early secondary school students.* Madison, WI: Center on Organization and Restructuring of Schools.

Lewis, N. (2001). Three foundations give $30 million to create small schools in New York City. *The Chronicle of Philanthropy, 8*(6), 22.

Littky, D., Allen, F., & Barth, R. (Eds.) (in press). *The schoolhouse is the place.* San Francisco: Jossey-Bass.

Littky, D., & Fried, R. (1988, January). The challenge to make good schools great. *National Education Association Journal,* pp. 4–8.

Marzano, R. J., Kendall, J. S., & Gaddy, B. B. (1999). *Essential knowledge: The debate over what American students should know.* Aurora, CO: Mid-continent Regional Educational Laboratory.

MacDonald, J. P., Smith, S., Turner, D., Finney, M., & Barton, E. (1993). *Graduation by exhibition: Assessing genuine achievement.* Alexandria, VA: Association for Supervision and Curriculum Development.

McGrath, M. (Senior Producer). (2000, October 11). *The Connection.* Boston, MA: WBUR Radio. (Available: http://www.theconnection.org/archive/2000/10/1011a.shtml)

Meier, D. (1995). *The power of their ideas: Lessons from a small school in Harlem*. Boston: Beacon Press.

Meier, D. (2000). *Will standards save public education? A New Democracy forum*. Boston: Beacon Press.

Moffett, J. (1994). *The universal schoolhouse: Spiritual awakening through education*. San Francisco: Jossey-Bass.

Muncey, D. E., & McQuillan, P. J. (1996). *Reform and resistance in schools and classrooms: An ethnographic view of the Coalition of Essential Schools*. New Haven, CT: Yale University Press.

Murnane, R. J., & Levy, F. (1996a). Evidence from fifteen schools in Austin, Texas. In G. Burtless (Ed.), *Does money matter? The effect of school resources on student achievement* (pp. 93–96). Washington, DC: Brookings Institution Press.

Murnane, R. J., & Levy, F. (1996b). *Teaching the new basic skills: Principles for educating children to thrive in a changing economy*. New York: The Free Press.

National Association of Secondary School Principals. (1996). *Breaking ranks: Changing an American institution*. Reston, VA: Author.

National Center for Education Statistics. (1999). *The condition of education*. Washington, DC: Office of Educational Research and Improvement.

National Research Council. (1999). *High stakes: Testing for tracking, promotion, and graduation*. Washington, DC: National Academy Press.

Nave, B., Miech, E., & Mosteller, F. (1998). *A rare design: The role of field trials in evaluating school practices*. Paper presented to the Evaluation Task Force of the Harvard Children's Initiative, Cambridge, MA.

Ohanian, S. (1999). *One size fits few: The folly of educational standards*. Portsmouth, NH: Heinemann.

Owen, D., with Doerr, M. (1999). *None of the above: The truth behind the SATs, revised edition*. Lanham, MD: Rowman & Littlefield.

Powell, A. G. (in progress). *Interests of mind: Mapping the territory*. Unpublished manuscript.

Powell, A. G., Farrar, E., & Cohen, D. K. (1985). *The shopping mall high school: Winners and losers in the educational marketplace*. Boston: Houghton Mifflin.

Public Education Fund. (1993). *Imagine: The report of the PROBE (Providence Blueprint for Education) Commission*. Providence, RI: Author.

Rhode Island Department of Education. (1999). *SALT survey: High performance learning community assessment*. Providence, RI: National Center on Public Education and Social Policy.

Rhode Island Department of Education. (2000a). *Information works! Measuring Rhode Island schools for change 2000*. Providence, RI: Author.

Rhode Island Department of Education. (2000b). *Ethnicity report for public school teachers.* Unpublished raw data.

Rose, M. (1989). *Lives on the boundary: A moving account of the struggles and achievements of America's educationally underprepared.* New York: Penguin Books.

Sarason, S. B. (1998). *Charter schools: Another flawed educational reform?* New York: Teachers College Press.

Schorr, L. B. (1997). *Common purpose: Strengthening families and neighborhoods to rebuild America.* New York: Doubleday.

Schorr, L. B., & Yankelovich, D. (2000, February 18). In search of a gold standard for social programs. *The Boston Globe,* p. A15.

Secretary's Commission on Achieving Necessary Skills (SCANS). (1991). *What work requires of schools: A SCANS report for America 2000.* Washington, DC: U.S. Department of Labor.

Sizer, T. (1984). *Horace's compromise: The dilemma of the American high school.* Boston: Houghton-Mifflin.

Sizer, T. (1996). *Horace's hope: What works for the American high school.* Boston: Houghton-Mifflin.

Sizer, T. (1999). No two are quite alike. *Educational Leadership, 57*(1), 6–11.

Steen, L. A. (Ed.) (1997). *Why numbers count: Quantitative literacy for tomorrow's America.* New York: College Entrance Examination Board.

Steinberg, A. (in press). *Forty-three valedictorians: Graduates of the Met talk about their learning.* Providence, RI: Northeast and Islands Regional Educational Laboratory.

Stiefel, L., Berne, R., Iatarola, P., & Fruchter, N. (2000). High school size: Effects on performance and budgets in New York City. *Educational Evaluation and Policy Analysis, 22*(1), 27–39.

U.S. Department of Education. (2000). *Fiscal Year 2000: Major initiatives and funding opportunities.* Washington, DC: Author.

Tyack, D. B., & Cuban, L. (1995). *Tinkering toward utopia: A century of public school reform.* Cambridge, MA: Harvard University Press.

Walker, E., & MacDonald, J. (1996). *Documentation/evaluation of the Rhode Island project, interim report to The Big Picture Company.* Providence, RI: The Big Picture Company.

Washor, E. (1999). Beyond hands-on learning. *High School Magazine, 6*(6), 34–35.

Wilson, F. (1998). *The hand: How its use shapes the brain, language, and human culture.* New York: Pantheon.

Wolk, R. (1998, November 18). Strategies for fixing failing public schools. Forum section. *Education Week,* p. 3.

Index

About the Author

Eliot Levine earned his doctorate in psychology from the University of Maryland and his bachelor's degree in electrical engineering and psychology from MIT. He has worked as a psychologist and education researcher at Harvard University, and he is preparing to become a high school teacher. He lives in Rhode Island with his wife, son, and foster daughter. He welcomes your feedback at elevine@alum.mit.edu.